D0564089

BEYOND
EASY
BELIEVISM

BEYOND EASY BELIEVISM

Gary R. Collins

WORD BOOKS
PUBLISHER
WACO, TEXAS

A DIVISION OF
WORD, INCORPORATED

BEYOND EASY BELIEVISM

Copyright © 1982 by Word, Inc.

All rights reserved. No part of this book may be reproduced in any form whatsoever, except for brief quotations in reviews, without the written permission of the publisher.

Library of Congress Cataloging in Publication Data

Collins, Gary R.
  Beyond easy believism.

  Includes bibliographical references and index.
  1. Christian life—1960–   I. Title.
BV4501.2.C6428 1982   248.4   82-11036
ISBN 0-8499-0332-7

Unless otherwise indicated, all Scripture quotations are from the New American Standard Bible (NASB), copyright © 1960, 1962, 1963, 1968, 1971 by The Lockman Foundation. Used by permission.

Quotations from the New International Version of the Bible (NIV) published by The Zondervan Corporation, are copyright © 1973 by New York Bible Society International.

Quotations marked LB are from *The Living Bible, Paraphrased* (Wheaton: Tyndale House Publishers, 1971) and are used by permission.

Printed in the United States of America

To those brothers and sisters
in Christ
who seek to resist the subtle tug
toward easy believism

"If anyone would come after me, he must deny himself and take up his cross daily and follow me. For whoever wants to save his life will lose it, but whoever loses his life for me will save it. What good is it for a man to gain the whole world, and yet lose or forfeit his very self? If anyone is ashamed of me and my words, the Son of Man will be ashamed of him when he comes in his glory and in the glory of the Father and of the holy angels. I tell you the truth, some who are standing here will not taste death before they see the kingdom of God. . . . No one who puts his hand to the plow and looks back is fit for service in the kingdom of God."

The words of Jesus in Luke 9:23–27, 62 (NIV)

Contents

Preface

The older I get, and the further I progress in my spiritual and intellectual pilgrimage, the more I am impressed with what can be learned from other writers.

A. W. Tozer, for example, was a prolific writer. His books, articles, editorials, and published sermons have continued to influence readers, even though he died in 1963.

Tozer once wrote that:

> The work of a good book is to incite the reader to moral action, to turn his eyes toward God and urge him forward. Beyond that it cannot go![1]

What a challenge for any writer. How I would hope that the volume which you hold in your hands could incite you to moral action, turn your eyes to God, and urge you forward in your spiritual and psychological growth.

This book took almost three years to complete. It began in a small-group Bible study when one of the participants began to wonder, out loud, whether Christians could really live a separated life style in the business and professional hurly-burly of the late twentieth century. The question lodged in my mind and motivated me to do some intense and prolific reading on questions about commitment, life style, and true spirituality. After a few months, I began to formulate conclusions which were presented tentatively to some of my friends, and later to church and student groups. As the ideas became clearer, I presented them in a lecture series at Barrington College in Rhode Island, shared them with some audiences in Australia, and refined them in several local church settings.

Once I began putting the ideas on paper, however, I began to wonder if I had become so engrossed in *thinking* about how to grow spiritually that I had stopped *growing*. It was at this point that I came across the words of another author.

Writing from the quiet solitude of a Trappist Monastery, psychologist-priest Henri J. M. Nouwen observed:

> Writing about prayer is often very painful since it makes you so aware of how far away you are from the ideal you write about. People who read your ideas tend to think that your writings reflect your life. . . . Your readers . . . invite you and challenge you to live up to your own thoughts and insights.
>
> This week all I am reading and writing about is prayer. I am so busy with it and often so excited about it that I have no time left to pray, and when I pray, I feel more drawn to my ideas on prayer than to praying. . . .
>
> Every time some kind of insight comes to me, I find myself wondering how I can use it in a lecture, a sermon, or an article, and very soon I am far away from God and all wrapped up in my own preoccupations.[2]

How easy it would be for me to write a book about the Christian life style and then to fall into the easy-believism mentality which I criticize so consistently in the following pages. It is easy for any of us to read a book like this one and then to put it aside without making any serious effort to apply the ideas to our own lives. A book like this could incite the reader to moral action, turn his or her eyes toward God and urge us forward, but ultimately the reader—and the writer—must each decide if we are going to change in any way because of what we read.

A student once paid me the greatest compliment that any teacher could desire. This student said nothing about my lecture preparation or delivery, my writing style, or my counseling. Instead, he simply stated, "Gary, I think you are growing, and you seek to have your students grow with you!"

Writing this book has helped me to grow and I deeply desire that God will use it to help its readers grow along with the author.

In the development of this manuscript, many people have offered encouragement and suggestions. I have already mentioned the audiences of people who listened graciously and responded insightfully. In addition, Carol Hemmer, Joan Davis, and Steve Snyder helped in a variety of ways with preparation of the manuscript; the people at Word, Inc. showed their characteristic expertise and cooperation in getting the book into print; and my wife Julie went over every sentence with her usual care and insight. I didn't always appreciate her suggestions for improvement, but invariably they were helpful and the manuscript—and its author—are both much better because of her loving and perceptive input.

Ultimately, each of us must aim for the goal of honoring and pleasing God with our lives. Perhaps you will agree with the writer who stated that the "life pleasing to God is not found in a series of religious duties but in obedience."[3] Only when obedience becomes central in life can we grow beyond superficial religion and into the spiritual depth which characterizes the maturing Christian. Many problems with life style fall into place when an individual determines to obey Christ unconditionally and to the best of his or her ability.

It is my prayer that the following pages will stimulate you, first to re-examine your beliefs and ways of living, then to work at changing your life style in ways that will make it more pleasing to God.

BEYOND
EASY
BELIEVISM

> Realize this, that in the last days . . .
> men will be lovers of self . . . holding
> to a form of godliness, although they
> have denied its power . . .
>
> *2 Timothy 3:1–5*

1
Easy Believism

John Lennon was no ordinary musician.

Born amidst poverty in a working class district of England, forsaken in childhood by his father and without the benefit of any "higher education," Lennon nevertheless rose to a position of worldwide popularity and influence. He was honored by the Queen of England. His work was discussed in scholarly journals. But the friends who knew him said he was cocky, antiestablishment and satirical. His open involvement in psychedelic drugs, experiments in Eastern mysticism, and public disdain for conventional morality shocked his critics but endeared him to a rebellious generation whose disillusionments he both reflected and encouraged.

One night on the street in front of his New York apartment, 40-year-old John Lennon was shot dead—felled by an admirer whose deranged mind had led him to premeditated murder.

Within hours editorials, accolades and eulogies began pouring out from the media. Lennon was described as "a brilliant historian and critic of his life and times," "the driving force behind a revolution which shook the world" and "a true creative artist." Acclaimed as "a genuine intellect" and "a champion of peace and personal freedom," he also was seen as "an alien in an incredible and maddening world, trying to fight his way out to sanity."

Lennon's widow announced that there would be no funeral; simply a ten-minute period of silence to commemorate his memory and "pray for his soul." At the appointed hour the people gathered: in Liverpool, London, Chicago, Sydney and around the world. Over 100,000 people, including the mayor and civic leaders, gathered in New York's Central Park—near the place where Lennon had been shot. There was sadness, anger at the "senseless nature" of the death, and expressions of appreciation for the Lennon music.

But there was little hope!

John Lennon had once written a song summarizing his beliefs. "I don't believe in magic," the lyrics began, and neither did he believe in the Bible, tarot, Jesus, Kennedy, Buddha, mantras, yoga, kings or even the Beatles.

"I just believe in me," he wrote. "That's reality!"

That also could be a doctrinal statement; a concise summary of what millions like Lennon believe today.

The era in which we live has been called "one of the most religiously saturated periods in our history."[1] The sale of Bibles and religious literature abounds. Churches tend to be filled with worshipers. Television and radio evangelists have attracted millions of followers to what has been termed "the electronic church." Bible studies and religious discussion groups have sprung up around the world.

But the divorce rate also is increasing. Pornography is selling at a record rate. Crime is up and moral standards are down. Millions claim to believe in God, but at least in America the present appears to be the most decadent era of our history. Even among professing Christians the God of Abraham, Isaac, Jacob and Paul seems to have been replaced with worship of ourselves and the quest for personal happiness, pleasure, freedom, and possessions.

We want to believe in God's goodness, in God's blessings and in an afterlife, even for nonbelievers like John Lennon—but life is empty for many people. They exist and sometimes mourn, but without any purpose in the present or hope for the future. They believe only in themselves and claim "that's reality." They have no reason to expect an afterlife. Of all people, they are "most to be pitied."

Modern Religion

A few months before John Lennon's death, a public opinion poll in the United States asked an interesting question:

"Would you say that you have been 'born again' or have had a 'born again' experience—that is, a turning point in your life when you committed yourself to Christ?"

A "yes" answer was given by 34 percent of those polled. That's a figure which could translate into 50 million Americans who are 18 years of age or older—all claiming to have committed themselves to Christ.

It isn't surprising that a sensitive reporter asked pollster George Gallup why our society isn't better than it is, when so many people claim to have been born again. The pollster's response was revealing.

"I suppose if people really, truly believed in the physical resurrection of Christ, more of them would be in Calcutta working with Mother Teresa. . . . *There is a huge gap between mere belief, and real conviction and practice.*"[2]

Modern religion appears to be characterized more by "mere belief" than by "real conviction and practice." Many people have found that it is fashionable to be religious, socially acceptable to be a church member, and even prestigious to be considered "born again." When religion is widely tolerated and accepted, however, there is a danger that even sincere believers will slip into a form of Christianity which is convenient and so easy that it might be called "easy believism." In the pages of this book we will explore this modern religion in more detail, but let us begin by looking at its most disturbing characteristics.

Easy believism is not demanding. Several years ago a world famous psychiatrist named Karl Menninger wrote a book in which he asked: "Whatever became of sin?"[3] Arguing that mental suffering and anxiety often are symptoms of moral sickness and irresponsibility, Menninger urged his readers to bring back the old idea of sin. When we pretend that sin and morality do not exist, he wrote, "we sink to despairing helplessness." We can't deal with our guilt, can't explain evil, and have no reason to hope for the future.

But sin is an unpopular word. It arouses images of hellfire and brimstone sermons. It raises uncomfortable ideas about moral failure, guilt, condemnation and personal responsibility. So, even in many churches, the word "sin" has been replaced with less abrasive terms like "forgetfulness," "little white lies," "laxity" or "negative thinking."

Throughout this land there are churches pastored by dynamic communicators who avoid references to sin or failure, and who build their popular sermons around inspiring stories of personal triumph and the value of a positive mental attitude. These churches preach a religion which is easy, convenient, and comfortable. The idea of "sin" has vanished, and with it, words like "self-discipline," "commitment," "repentance," and "sacrifice" have disappeared from the vocabulary and thinking of many modern worshipers and their leaders. When there is no emphasis on repentance, and little emphasis on holiness and the Word of God, there is no true religion. Easy believism reigns instead.

Easy believism is not costly. Most of us are busy people with limited time and even less money. In self-defense, we have tended to surround ourselves with thick walls of resistance which are almost impervious to appeals for funds or requests for nonfinancial help. We become so skilled in spotting appeals for money that we throw away many of the letters unopened. At times we get annoyed when these same letters try to manipulate us with sad stories, pictures of unhappy kids with bloated stomachs, or the promise of gifts in return for our dollars. It is easy to resist when someone tries to make us feel guilty by reminding us that we have so much but people in the ghettos have so little. When the church has its "stewardship Sunday" many Christians prefer to stay away.

If these appeals were for worthless causes we could ignore them easily and throw away the letters without any further thought. Most of the requests which come to our mail boxes, however, present important financial needs. If you are like me, you would like to give to all these causes, but this isn't possible. To keep from feeling guilty, therefore, we find reasons to ignore them, to criticize them, and to carry on with our accustomed comfortable ways of life.

There is a danger that this kind of thinking can take over our attitudes toward Christianity. How easy it is to find "good" reasons and occasional excuses which allow us to say "no" when there is a request for our time, energies, abilities, or money. How comfortable and appealing it can be to recast Christianity into a self-centered form of philosophy which doesn't cost us anything and which doesn't interfere with our busy schedules.

Easy believism is socially acceptable. In his classic book on religious experience, William James wrote that religion can exist in our lives either as a dull habit or as an acute fever. When religion is a habit with little more than traditional rituals, it doesn't affect us much. If we take our beliefs seriously, however, and try to live a truly religious life, there is a possibility that we could be considered "exceptional and eccentric."[4] To prove that this can happen, James gave dozens of examples of deeply religious people who appeared to be unusual, peculiar, and so different that some considered them to be pathological.

I have often wondered how people would look at Jesus if he came to live on the earth in the late twentieth century. Even in the first century people recognized that he was different. He preached a message of love, refused to go along with the hypercritical religion of his time, and resisted the acclaim of the crowds. He called his disciples to leave the security of their homes and jobs to follow him where they would encounter persecution and resistance.

Such a message was not popular when Jesus preached it; it certainly is unpopular today, even among many Christians. We want to be "well adjusted" to our society. We want the world to know that Christians can be intellectual, up-to-date, successful and liberated. Most of us smile with a mixture of amusement and embarrassment when we see Christians whose beliefs lead them to wear special clothing, shun make-up, grow long beards or make unpopular political statements. In contrast, it is easier to blur any distinctions between the church and the world.

One reason for this acceptance of worldly standards is that we want nonbelievers to know that Christians can be stylish, socially acceptable and fun-loving. In our desire to make Christianity attractive, however, we rarely win men and women to Christ as we might hope. Instead we demonstrate to the nonbeliever that there is nothing unique about the Christian and before long we find ourselves embracing a socially acceptable but watered down "dull habit" form of Christianity.

Easy believism is self-centered. According to an old Greek legend, Narcissus was a young man whose rejection of the maiden Echo caused her to die of a broken heart. Nemesis, the god of revenge, punished Narcissus by making him fall in love with his own reflection in the pond. Eventually he pined away in self-admiration and was transformed into the narcissus, an early spring flower that nourished itself in water.

This quaint story is ancient fantasy, but it has given us the word "narcissism," which describes something modern and very real. Narcissism means the love of self. Narcissistic people are self-centered and often selfish. They tend to be immature—primarily concerned about their own well-being, happiness and personal fulfillment. According to Freud, all children are narcissistic—and many of us never change. We go through life "looking out for number one." We are fascinated with books or articles about self-fulfillment, self-actualization, and self-assertion. We hate to be inconvenienced, and we have trouble handling anything which delays or interferes with our self-centered plans.

This "me-centered" attitude appears to be the guiding philosophy of many people today. It is a religion which says, "I am the center of my universe. I don't want God telling me what to do. I can meet my own needs and take care of myself. I insist upon my civil rights, including the right to enjoy myself and to express myself. Absolutes are non-existent. I will determine my own standards of right and wrong. I will answer only to myself."[5]

Such a philosophy permeates television and movie programs. It can lead to increasing violence (which basically is self-centered), immorality, drug or alcohol abuse, white-collar crime, shoplifting and deception. It undermines families and can lead to arguments, physical abuse, desertion and divorce. Selfish narcissism is a guiding force in the worlds of politics, government, business, athletics, entertainment, education and the professions.[6] Is it surprising, therefore, that this same philosophy has permeated the church?

I don't suppose there is anything wrong with seeking a church where our needs are met and where we can worship in comfort. Personal fulfillment and comfort, however, often become the dominant themes of our worship services and small group discussions. We hear little about self-sacrifice or self-denial. Instead, testimonies, sermons and Christian self-help books proclaim the creed that life will be prosperous and personally happy if we pray enough, believe enough, or worship enough. If we are not careful, God becomes a magic genie who exists to satisfy our selfish desires and to bow in response to our personal whims. Positive mental attitude becomes our doctrine. "Believe in yourself and you'll get what you want" becomes our creed. This self-centered way of thinking is really a modern form of idolatry.

What in this life concerns you most? How you answer very likely indicates what you worship instead of Jesus Christ.[7] If thoughts of ourselves, our possessions or our own fulfillment occupy most of our attention, we have fallen into "idolatrous narcissism."[8] This is not the teaching of Jesus or of the New Testament writers, but it is a prominent characteristic of modern easy believism.

Easy believism seeks for pat answers. The Book of Job is a sensitive and insightful narrative about a man under stress. Reeling from the loss of his possessions, family, status, and health, Job turned to three friends who had come to bring comfort. The first gave a moral speech about why Job was suffering. The second gave a simplistic analysis of Job's troubles. The third criticized. None of the three listened to Job or really tried to understand his hurt and despair. Each had pat answers which were critical of Job and useless in helping him cope.

We Christians believe that "Christ is the answer" to human needs. Thus, when we encounter intense suffering, ruthless injustice, premature death, immorality in our leaders, or emotional illness and despair in fellow believers we often are confused and tongue-tied. Unconsciously we may fear that our theology does not have all the answers so, like Job's "comforters," we search for explanations. We decide, for example, that all mental illness results from personal sin or that God must think some people are "really special" since he has chosen to let them suffer so much. When we can't find a plausible explanation, we give advice, talk about more pleasant subjects, or quote Bible verses.

Wouldn't it be better to admit that sometimes we don't understand why people suffer? Wouldn't it be more honest to recognize that most of us really don't know what to say when we meet modern Jobs? God hasn't revealed all of his ways to us (Rom. 11:33) and even if he chose to do so our little minds could never understand completely. He doesn't need us to defend his ways and propose reasons to excuse his seemingly confusing actions. Finding pat answers is often a cover for our own insecurities and fears. It is a way to avoid the pain of suffering and the realization that we have limited understanding. Too often, it is a mark of modern religion.

Easy believism wants a certainty of success. Nobody likes to fail. We don't put our money into business ventures which probably won't succeed. We rarely enroll in training programs if it seems unlikely that we will graduate. We hope to avoid marriages that will end in divorce. We are a success-oriented people and in general this makes good sense.

It is not surprising, therefore, that a success mentality which controls our daily lives also colors our views of religion. Who wants a religion which promises failure? Why bother with a God unless we can be assured of fringe benefits like peace, health, happiness, and protection?

"Reverend Ike" is a flamboyant television evangelist who preaches that God doesn't want anybody to be poor. "Believe in him," this preacher proclaims repeatedly, "then you will believe in yourself, and if you believe in yourself you will get rich—like I am rich."

In more sophisticated forms, the same message is proclaimed from some of the most famous pulpits of our land. "God wants you to succeed!" "You can if you think you can!" "Nothing is impossible!" Such proclamations feed what has been called "our insurance mentality"[9]—the view that life must be reliable, predictable and safe. It is a message blatantly stated in a best selling book on depression written by a highly acclaimed Christian author. "Of one thing I am confident," he wrote. "You do not have to be depressed. . . . I am convinced that by using the formula in this book you can avoid every being depressed again."

Lest I be misunderstood let me hasten to add that the Bible does promise inner peace, joy, and an "abundant life" to those who follow Christ. Jesus did promise that he would never leave or forsake us and he left this earth after giving assurance that he had gone to prepare dwelling places for us in heaven. The Bible is filled with promises which are meant to be taken seriously.

But there is no biblical guarantee that Christians will be wealthy, free of illness or protected from depression. That is the mentality of easy believism.

In contrast, Jesus promised that his followers would have tribulation, persecution and rejection even from their own family members. He called on his followers to take up a cross and follow him who had no home and whose life ended with torture, a senseless trial, and execution. His predictions were exemplified in the life of Paul the apostle whose external pressures and inner turmoil are clearly recorded in Scripture (2 Cor. 11:24–28). A similar message shines forth from Hebrews 11 where we see a listing of the great giants of the faith. With God's help, some performed incredible feats; but others were mocked, beaten, imprisoned, deserted, and murdered.

Easy believism wants entertainment. I hesitate to include this because I don't want to believe that it really is true. But how many of us want church to be a place where we can be entertained? We go not as worshipers to a sanctuary, but as spectators to an auditorium. Accustomed to spectacular productions on television, we want our church services to be the same. We have spotlights, roving microphones, and "big sound" orchestral backgrounds to our music—all of which can be good, but each of which tends to be compared with the "real thing" on TV. If the sermon is dull or not spiced with anecdotes and humor, if the music is second class or if the evening church service isn't interesting, we stay at home or criticize—like drama reviewers coldly and objectively evaluating a play. We've even introduced coffee breaks and installed air conditioning to make the entertainment center more attractive.

It would be dishonest if I implied that none of this interested me. I like the coffee breaks (and occasionally even help in serving the coffee). I believe that refreshment times can do much to draw people together for fellowship and mutual support. Concerts can be genuinely uplifting and often give us a reason for inviting nonbelievers who otherwise would not attend church. I appreciate good church music and condone neither boring ritual nor poorly prepared sermons.

We must recognize, however, that worship involves the adoration of a holy and supreme God who wants our praise, confession, and commitment. Caught up in the entertainment mentality of our culture, there is real danger that we will let our church services degenerate into "show-biz" performances, built around "superstar" personalities, watched with sharp criticism, and evaluated with applause or silent booing.

Easy believism shuns authority. We are a people who love independence and revere freedom. We don't want others telling us what to do and we are reluctant to say anything which might squelch or violate human rights.

In a thought-provoking statement, Soviet exile Alexander Solzhenitsyn has concluded that in the West, the defense of individual rights has reached such extremes as to make society as a whole defenseless against certain individuals . . . . Destructive and irresponsible freedom has been granted boundless space. Society appears to have little defense against the abyss of human decadence, such as, for example, misuse of liberty for moral violence against young people, motion pictures full of pornography, crime and horror.[10]

We have so idolized freedom and shunned authority that our society seems to be in danger of degenerating into chaos and anarchy. We could become like the nation which was described by one poignant sentence in the Old Testament: "In those days there was no king in Israel; everyone did what was right in his own eyes" (Judg. 21:25).

How do we Christians respond to such a way of thinking? Often we join the crowd and proclaim limitless freedom for everyone. We build both our morals and our sermons on the existence of "love"—as each person defines this individually.

Even when the Bible is taken seriously we are reluctant to make proclamations which sound dogmatic or authoritative. We spend more time talking about the Bible than reading and seeking to apply its words. Justifiably we criticize those scholars who use biblical criticism to set themselves up as censors, deciding which parts of the Bible are true and which should be rejected. Regretfully, we do the same thing using "selective hermeneutics"[11]—an approach to Bible study which lets us emphasize and believe what we want while we ignore the rest.

British theologian J. I. Packer is close to the truth when he writes that at no time since the Reformation have Christians as a group been so "unsure, tentative and confused" as to what they should believe and how they should act.

> The outside observer sees us as staggering on from gimmick to gimmick . . . like so many drunks in a fog, not knowing at all where we are or which way we should be going. Preaching is hazy; heads are muddled; hearts fret; doubts drain our strength; uncertainty paralyzes action[12]

primarily because we have selfishly and arrogantly refused to accept and submit to the authority of the Bible as the Word of God.

The erosions of biblical authority along with the other characteristics of easy believism are subtle in their influence. Gradually, and often without conscious awareness, many of us slip into the modern religion which characterizes our culture. We worship in our churches, tithe our money, mouth the same old clichés, and fail to recognize that we have become lukewarm devotees of a worthless religion. Like the ancient Laodiceans who thought they were spiritually alive, rich, and in need of nothing, we are wretched, miserable, poor, blind, and naked.

The Origins of Easy Believism

A number of perceptive writers have tried to understand why we so easily slip into easy believism. A Canadian critic named Pierre Berton has argued that the church, like society, is too comfortable. We have become fossilized and unable to speak to the needs of contemporary people.[13] A more recent writer has proposed that religion in our time has been captured by the "tourist mindset." Like vacationers, we visit church to see a new personality, hear a new idea, have a new experience or in some other way bring diversion into our boring lives.[14] Others have suggested that instead of taking clear moral leadership, the church has been molded by its culture. As a result we have developed the same confusion and loss of identity that individuals experience in our unstable modern society.

Like the Trojan horse, a devastating force has infiltrated our churches and has been gnawing away at our minds. That force is atheistic humanism—the belief that human beings are the center of all things. Humanism believes in human goodness and potential, resists absolute standards of right or wrong, and concludes that human beings are sovereign and alone in a universe that is without any God. With brilliant clarity Solzhenitsyn described this force in his famous address at Harvard University.

> A tilt of freedom in the direction of evil has come about gradually, but it was evidently born primarily out of a humanistic and benevolent concept according to which there is no evil inherent in human nature; the world belongs to mankind and all the defects of life are caused by wrong social systems which must be corrected.[15]

The widespread growth of "humanism without its Christian heritage," continued Solzhenitsyn, has led to a loss of courage in the West, a decline in morals, a superficiality in our thinking, and a lack of commitment to any cause. We assume that human beings are able to control their own destiny, but forget that we are never free of pride, self-interest, envy, and a variety of other defects which undermine our efforts at self-improvement.

It is easy for Christians to read these words, to admit that we have known this all along, and then to conclude smugly that *we* are unspotted by secular humanistic beliefs. But the prevalence of easy believism even among believers challenges that conclusion.

In the Epistle of James, the writer warns against worthless religion. This may be pure theologically but it rarely results in changed lives or compassionate actions. Instead of an easy believism based on contemporary humanism, we are urged to find a religion which is pure and faultless. Such religion involves a willingness to hear and do what God commands in his Word. It is a religion characterized by acts of compassion and by holy living in which we keep ourselves "unstained by the world" (James 1:22, 27).

On a long airplane flight one day I found myself seated next to a businessman with whom I struck up a casual conversation. In answer to my query he described his work and I, in turn, indicated that I was both a psychologist and a Christian.

"Maybe you can answer a question for me," he suggested. "Do you know what it means to be born again?" This question forced me to think through the meaning of a familiar term.

My fellow passenger had never heard of Nicodemus, the educated ruler who came to Jesus with a similar question. In his reply, Jesus stated that people in this world love darkness rather than light. Their deeds are evil. They do not really believe that Jesus is the Son of God who came to save us from our self-centered thinking. These nonbelievers are judged and condemned already (John 3:18).

But the Good News is that God loved the world and gave his Son so that anyone who believes in him will not perish but have eternal life (John 3:16).

The new birth comes when we yield ourselves completely to Christ and trust him to forgive our sins and guide our actions. The new birth is an inner spiritual transformation which comes when Christ enters our lives. We don't earn this new status by our efforts or by good works; it is a gift from God bestowed freely on all who ask him for it (Eph. 2:8,9). It may involve elation but it is more than an emotional high. Those who want to be born again are freely received and brought into a personal relationship with Jesus Christ.

Such people are truly born again—into God's family. They have become God's children because they have committed themselves to him.

At the beginning, perhaps, this new birth is "mere belief," but the sincere child of God begins to develop "real conviction and practice." Frequently, we are tempted to slip into an easy believism—that modern form of religion built on atheistic humanism—and at times most of us give in to the temptation. But God gently prods us and encourages us to "grow in the grace and knowledge of our Lord and Savior Jesus Christ" (2 Peter 3:18). Slowly our lives become a reflection, not of worthless religion but of a dynamic spirituality.

This is pure and faultless religion. It involves a growing relationship with Jesus Christ which goes beyond easy believism. It is identified by at least the ten characteristics which we will discuss, one at a time, in the chapters which follow.

> If anyone wishes to come after Me, let
> him deny himself, and take up his cross
> daily, and follow Me. . . . No one,
> after putting his hand to the plow and
> looking back, is fit for the kingdom of
> God.
>
> *Luke 9:23, 62*

2

Costly Commitment

My mailbox recently contained a disturbing request. Would it be possible, a letter asked, for me to join the advisory board of an organization which had been created to publish "professionally and attractively produced clothbound" volumes containing the names and biographies of America's most noteworthy evangelical leaders? It appeared that this invitation was sincere and I did not want to discourage anyone who was "truly excited about the bright prospects" of producing a six-volume "Who's Who Among Evangelicals."

But I turned down the invitation—almost immediately.

I didn't question the motives of the two strangers who had written the letter. Their vision in trying to honor the work of Christian leaders was admirable, but in rereading their letter about the project, I felt that, perhaps without even realizing it, they were trying to enlist my help by making flattering comments. That is a common way of motivating others, but it boosts egos and sometimes can be blatantly manipulative. It also reflects the emphasis on celebrities which seems to dominate our society.

Within recent years, approximately 450 "Who's Who" publications have been printed and in America alone there are over 750 separate halls of fame. The rest of the world has only three![1] We like to honor the famous and perhaps we unconsciously share in their success as we give them acclaim. Thousands of readers devour magazine articles about people who are important enough to be unique or visible while fan mail pours in to some celebrities by the ton. Without giving it much thought, perhaps many of us accept the secular conclusion that in this world, worth and fame go together. If you're not at least a little famous, you're a nobody; you can only find real significance by becoming a star or by convincing yourself that you are a friend of the famous. Politicians, restauranteurs, and even some Christian leaders like to be photographed with famous people, and then line their walls both with these photographs and with autographed pictures from celebrities.

Our fascination with important people tends to divide us into two separate castes, the "well-known" and the "unknown." The unknown (the majority of us) sometimes feel unimportant and, at least in the younger years, are driven by an urge to become successful and visible. In contrast I have heard that many well-known people live with the threat of losing their hard-earned popularity. To maintain their images and to protect themselves from admiring fans, these celebrities withdraw into a glittering but unreal world. Many actually take the accolades at face value and soon lose contact with the refreshing realities of common life. This, in turn, can dull their creativity and lead to disillusionment and destructive pride.[2]

If all of this preoccupation with fame stopped at the church door it would be harmful enough, but many Christians also seem to have embraced the celebrity-worship mentality. We take special delight in the conversions of show-business, athletic and political personalities. Ignoring Paul's warning, we rush to "lay hands" on born-again celebrities so we can push them to prominence at mass rallies or in front of Christian talk show cameras. To satisfy our hunger for prominence, we create heroes of our own by lauding Christian musicians, authors, and even an occasional preacher or seminar leader.

How inconsistent this is with Jesus' radical teaching that the truly great people in this world are servants (Matt. 20:26)—some of whom may be famous but most of whom will be unknown! How different is "celebrityism" from the biblical teaching that we are to avoid giving special honor to some members of the body of Christ while we heap second-class status on others (1 Cor. 12:13–27;

James 2:9). How dangerous can be the tendency to boast, not "in the Lord" (1 Cor. 1:31), but in Christian celebrities who are immortalized by Christian halls of fame, self-centered autobiographies and books of evangelical "who's who" personalities.

Most dangerous of all, perhaps, is the temptation for us to conclude that Christianity, as demonstrated by celebrities, doesn't involve any cost or sacrifice. The celebrity mentality subtly teaches that although

> Jesus wants you to be happy, it takes a lot to be happy. Not only are wealth and beauty and fame prerequisites for true happiness, but . . . besides these things you need Jesus. Then you will have it all . . . . Life will become the spiritual orgasm God intended it to be.[3]

Such thinking overlooks the fact that Jesus called for radical changes in the life styles of the people whom he met. He told sinners to stop committing adultery. Others were expected to change their professions and forsake their income-producing jobs. A few were faced with the fact that their religion would create tension at home, and some were instructed to sell everything and give the money to the poor. Never did Jesus tell anyone to "follow me, but stay just the way you are."[4]

Staying the way you are is a reaction to life which many modern people embrace. It is well known that our generation has been called the "me first" era, in which many individuals are committed primarily to self-enhancement, self-indulgence and self-satisfaction. One observer has suggested that the two most influential men of this century have been Elvis Presley and Hugh Hefner. As leaders of a moral revolution they directed millions into a passive acceptance of self-centered hedonism.

Now, however, this self-centered way of thinking may be giving way to a "postponing" mentality in which people handle decisions by avoiding them. The future is too frightening to think about. Commitment to anything—be it God, country, spouse, career or friends—is too threatening and inconvenient to ponder.[5] It is easier to put off until tomorrow what should be done today. As this philosophy becomes more prevalent, we see increasing numbers of people wandering through adulthood with little purpose in life and no direction. It isn't surprising that we look with awe on the famous people who seem to have suceeded in life.

In the midst of the campus upheavals in the 1960s, a federal cabinet minister in the United States government wrote a message which still applies both to his countrymen and to people in other nations:

> We fall into the error of thinking that happiness necessarily involves ease, diversion, tranquility (and fame)—a state in which all of one's wishes are satisfied. In most people, happiness is not to be found in this vegetative state but in *striving toward meaningful goals. . . .* I believe that most Americans would welcome a new burst of moral commitment and an end to the apathy, indifference and disengagement which have crept over the nation. The best kept secret in America today is that people would rather work hard for something they believe in than enjoy a pampered idleness.[6]

In a series of crisp and concise word pictures, the Bible (in Hebrews 11) shows an impressive parade of godly heroes who were neither pampered nor idle. Some were famous; many were unknown among their contemporaries. Some were rich; others lived in poverty. While many saw God work miracles, others were forced to live with sickness, pain, rejection, torture or obscurity.

And what made all of these people great? They all had faith in God and were courageous enough to stand firmly by their convictions, even when this meant being different.

Such commitment rarely has been prized in our day of celebrity worship. "If we no longer have any heroes," wrote an observer in *Harper's* magazine, "it may not be because no one is fit to be a hero, but because we are not fit to recognize one."[7] Impressed as we are by the succession of "big name" and glamorous superstars, we are reluctant to acknowledge or honor those truly unusual people who might not be famous but whose dedication and sincerity might disturb or challenge those of us who seem less committed. We are uncomfortable in the presence of potential heroes whose words and example might call us to effort, duty, sacrifice, or even to a willingness to let God determine who is to become well known and who will remain in obscurity.

The People of Commitment

Several years ago I had lunch with a traveling evangelist who saw his name and picture on billboards, buses and bumper stickers whenever he came to town for a series of preaching meetings.

"At first it bothered me," my friend observed, "but now I accept it as a way to both develop interest and attract people to the meetings."

Then he made an interesting statement.

"In our society, people rarely follow ideas or ideals. People follow people!"

The apostle Paul must have reached that same conclusion. He instructed readers to be like him, and in one place stated bluntly: "Be imitators of me just as I also am of Christ" (1 Cor. 11:1). Paul was not proposing hero worship. Surely he resisted the creation of celebrities, but he knew that to a large degree we become like the people whom we most admire. For this reason, there is wisdom in the old advice that we should take time to choose our models carefully.

Of all the people in the Bible, whom do you admire most? When you consider people who have lived in your lifetime, who are your real heroes? Are there Christians living now or in the past whom you sincerely esteem? Do you have some non-Christian models who truly are admirable? How you answer these questions may say something about your own values and priorities. Your answers also will reflect what really is important to you.

Three or four years ago I would not have included Corrie ten Boom in my list of heroes. C. S. Lewis would have been there, along with Paul Tournier, Billy Graham and one or two others. But I knew little about the ten Boom family until I worked on a project involving *The Hiding Place*—a movie which told the story of Corrie ten Boom's life during World War II. I had a copy of the film in my home and saw it perhaps fifteen or twenty times. I read books by and about Corrie ten Boom and came away permanently influenced by one outstanding characterstic of the ten Boom family. They had a solid and unwavering commitment to Jesus Christ.

The life experiences of the ten Booms are now very familiar. Born and raised in Holland, Corrie and her sister Betsie were unmarried, unknown, middle-aged women when the Nazi influence spread across Europe. Throughout their whole lives the ten Boom family had been so deeply committed to helping others that it was natural for them to protect and hide some of the persecuted Jews who were being hunted by Hitler's agents in the Netherlands.

One day the ten Booms were arrested and abruptly hauled off to a prison camp. Conditions were indescribably severe—far worse,

Corrie ten Boom said later, than anything that could be depicted in a film. Old Papa ten Boom soon died and Betsie passed away several months later. Other family members were killed or their health so badly deteriorated that life ended prematurely. The ten Boom commitment had been costly but despite the pain and apparently without much hesitation, the family members had stood firm in their beliefs even when this meant danger, inconvenience, obscurity and the probability of death.

Corrie ten Boom may never have read the writings of Dietrich Bonhoeffer, but she would have agreed with some of his conclusions. Like the ten Booms, Bonhoeffer also was arrested by the Nazis and sent to a prison camp just a few years after he had written his now famous comments about "cheap grace":

> Cheap grace is the preaching of forgiveness without requiring repentance, baptism without church discipline, communion without confession, absolution without personal confession. Cheap grace is grace without discipleship, grace without the cross, grace without Jesus Christ, living and incarnate . . . .
> It is under the influence of this kind of "grace" that the world has been made "Christian," but at the cost of secularizing the Christian religion as never before . . . . The Christian life comes to mean nothing more than living in the world and as the world, in being no different from the world, in fact, in being prohibited from being different from the world for the sake of grace. The upshot of it all is that my duty as a Christian is to leave the world for an hour or so on a Sunday morning and go to church to be assured that my sins are all forgiven. I need no longer try to follow Christ, for cheap grace, the bitterest foe of discipleship . . . has freed me from that.[8]

Cheap grace sounds a lot like easy believism. It is a Christianity without cost or commitment. It sees religion as a personal hobby or an "extra" experience which does little more than add zest and interest to life. Such superficial faith could never have sustained a Corrie ten Boom or a Dietrich Bonhoeffer during their times of intense physical suffering. The heroes of Hebrews 11 would have buckled under if their faith had involved nothing more than a casual commitment to easy believism. The thousands of believers who suffer today in Iron-Curtain prison camps do not maintain their stability and convictions because they have only a cheap grace.

We who live in the free world are permitted to worship as we wish, but even here there can be tension and criticism because of our beliefs. Students who openly state their beliefs about creation, business people who take a stand for honesty, employees who are determined to put in a full day's work or to resist injustice at work, politicians or church leaders who take a stand for what they believe to be right, young people who resist the pressures to slip into immorality—these are among the people in our midst who encounter ridicule, ostracism, and sometimes unemployment or persecution because of their commitments.

The research of social psychologists has demonstrated that people are more committed to those things for which they have to suffer. "Faith is nurtured by commitment," writes David Myers. "How many Christians, nurtured on a religion of success and positive thinking"—perhaps mixed with a dose of celebrity worship— "would stand by their faith if it implied suffering and despisement rather than social and economic success?"[9] Surely if we emphasized the cost of discipleship, like Jesus did, thousands of nominal believers would quickly jump off the "born again" bandwagon.

The Resistance to Commitment

Tolerance has become a prized virtue in contemporary society. Almost ignored by Bible writers, tolerance nevertheless dominates much of modern thinking and gives us an excuse for not expressing our beliefs or revealing our feelings. Nobody wants to be considered intolerant so many of us let others express their opinions while we maintain a noncommital neutrality.

Douglas Hooker has suggested that in many cases "the person who is tolerant prefers to avoid any situation where he is expected to reveal his real feelings." Regardless of how attractive or repulsive we may find a relationship with another person, it is easier to react in a manner that is pleasantly neutral, and which thus removes the possibility that a personal commitment could bring conflict with others.[10] It is more comfortable to remain neutral, or at least to hide one's commitments, than to reveal what we believe and thus to risk criticism.

Commitment which is hidden, however, is not really commitment. The degree of a person's commitment can be gauged by the actions and determination shown as that person seeks to attain a goal. Undoubtedly it is true that words speak louder than inner thoughts, and that actions speak louder than words. What we do often is the clearest indication of our real values and beliefs.

Why then, do many people have stated commitments which are so weak that they never spill forth into action? Perhaps the major answer centers around the word *fear*. If we commit ourselves to a course of action or express an inner conviction, we might get criticism and there is a possibility that we will fail or be proven wrong. This fear of failure or ostracism can immobilize us. So we do nothing and convince ourselves that we really are being "open" and tolerant. This way of thinking can become ingrained in an unhealthy way. The

> . . . noncommitter holds onto the very special myth about his own invincibility and high potentiality. He believes he could do many things if only he were really to go all out, but he chooses instead to bide his time, waiting for the right day and opportunity to come along. The longer he delays, the more important the myth becomes to his self-esteem and the greater is his reluctance to take the risk of discovering that it may have no basis in fact. . . . He becomes trapped. . . .[11]

But there is a way out of this trap. We can hear the views of others—with an attitude of respect and sincere tolerance—but without feeling the obligation to agree. We can recognize that real commitment involves an attempt to understand others and to be actively involved in their lives. Then we can ask for God's help so that we may be able to express our beliefs graciously, set our life goals carefully and plan our actions realistically.

The apostle Paul was a man of conviction who expressed himself clearly, was involved with others compassionately and set goals realistically. These human involvements and goals were not rigid or solely human. They were made in the spirit of Proverbs 16:9: "The mind of man plans his way. But the Lord directs his steps." Such an attitude says, "Lord, this is what we believe you want us to do, and this is what we intend to do. If you would like to direct us into another path, we are open to your leading. Meanwhile we move ahead in faith."[12] Such a perspective gets us moving but keeps us both from rigidity and from the fear of committing ourselves to some course of action.

The Meaning of Commitment

In all of the Old Testament there probably is no story more familiar than that of Daniel in the lion's den. In my mind, I can still see a familiar Sunday school picture showing Daniel, clad in a long brown monklike dress with a rope tied around his middle, standing in the midst of sleeping lions who look no more dangerous than the stone beasts which guard the entrance to our local art gallery. When I was a child, the story of Daniel was repeated often but for me it was little more than a fascinating tale from some bygone era of history.

Only after I reached adulthood did the full impact of that man's commitment begin to permeate my mind. Daniel had been snatched from his home and enrolled in a three-year training program designed to prepare him for the king's personal service. The training must have been demanding but from the beginning this young man decided to stand firm in his commitment to God. When given the opportunity to interpret royal dreams, Daniel clearly stated that his abilities came from God. When he saw hardship and destruction ahead, he was courageous enough to declare this message boldly even though such honesty could have led to immediate death. When he was given acclaim, he refused to let comfortable celebrity status lure him away from his convictions and into compromise with the humanism of that day. Daniel was a true hero who knew what he believed and who stood firm in his commitment to God.

Commitment is like that. It involves *making a firm decision to abide by some rule or standard.* When Daniel first entered the royal court he made up his mind that he would not eat the king's rich food or drink the fine wines (Dan. 1:8). Having committed himself to that guideline, Daniel knew what to do when he was offered the royal delicacies. He politely refused to eat and asked for simpler fare.

It could be argued that such commitments can make us rigid and tense, but the making of firm decisions can also reduce pressure.[13] The person who is committed to marriage, for example, can avoid many costly and painful experiences because of this commitment. There is no flirting with strangers, no looking around for better options, no pleading for divorce—marriage has become a firm decision to love and cherish until death. Because we have made firm commitments, decisions can be easier and life can be less stressful. Life is much more difficult when we have no commitments or when others can easily persuade us to change our commitments.

Such wavering is a characteristic of easy-believism. When decisions about values, beliefs, and standards are not held firmly, we tend to shift our positions whenever something new appears, or whenever we are criticized or challenged. We justify such shifting viewpoints by inventing excuses and talking about wanting to be relevant and flexible.

In the court of King Darius, Daniel once heard a decree to worship the king or face death. Because of his commitment to God, Daniel ignored the new law and was thrown to lions who were truly fierce and ravenously hungry. Under similar circumstances today would many of us find a convenient rationalization which would let us appear to bow before the king to save our own necks?

Elton Trueblood surely is correct in his assertion that while churches are filled and growing, committed Christians are in a minority at the present time.[14] If we understood and accepted the importance of "making firm decisions" about our Christian standards, beliefs, and actions, there would be no need for books which call us to commitment or describe what a company of committed believers is really like.[15]

The Core of Commitment

The Epistle of James contains some of the most practical guidance that we can find in the Bible. On first reading, it may seem that James has given separate pearls of practical wisdom tied together with no pattern or direction. But the book does have a theme strung throughout its five short chapters. It is a call to unwavering commitment in response both to suffering and to the easy-believism type of hypocrisy which has distracted believers since the time of Christ.

Commitment involves listening to the Word of God. In our day we are more inclined to criticize and explain away the Bible than to listen to its teachings. Christian counselors see this frequently when their clients present intriguing and sometimes plausible reasons for ignoring God's Word and continuing in their worldly ways. Christian writers, like James A. Packer, have tried to analyze this drift toward a casual and sometimes judgmental attitude concerning the Bible. Perhaps all of us, at times, ignore the Scriptures or set ourselves above it, "acting as if we already knew its contents inside out, and were indeed in a position to fault it as being neither wholly safe nor wholly sound as a guide to the ways of God." If such attitudes get a foothold we lose faith in the Bible's credibility. When that happens "we have also lost touch with God's law and Gospel, His commandments and His promises, and indeed with His Christ."[16]

Is it surprising, then, that so many people feel unsure, tentative, and confused about their beliefs and standards of right or wrong? How can anyone develop a clear faith if he or she fails to take God's Word seriously? How can we claim that the Bible is important if we are unable to fit studying it into our busy schedules?

James doesn't instruct us to read and understand the Bible; he simply assumes that the believer would be doing that. We will, he supposes, be hearing the Word, looking at it intensely, and learning from the wisdom which God has revealed in Scripture.

Commitment involves obedience to the Word of God. Even if we read the Bible and the Holy Spirit helps us to understand, we can still remain in a state of easy-believism emptiness if we fail to obey scriptural teaching. The devil himself knows and understands the Bible (he used this knowledge extensively during the temptation of Jesus), but he does not obey it. Like some modern theologians who view the Bible as an interesting specimen to be observed and dissected, any one of us can slip into a dead orthodoxy if we understand theology and scriptural teaching but fail to let it permeate and change our lives. Such a preoccupation with study, wrote Kierkegaard, can become a way of keeping the Word from speaking to us directly; an excuse for not doing what the Bible clearly instructs.[17]

James is explicit about this. Too often, he writes, we become "merely hearers" who will ourselves into a false sense of security because we are content simply to understand what is written without applying it to our lives. That is like looking at our faces in the mirror, seeing what needs to be done to change our appearance, and then walking away without doing anything. In contrast, James firmly asserts that we must be "effectual doers" and not simply "forgetful hearers" of divine teaching (James 1:22–25).

Perhaps "obedience" is one of the most unpopular words in modern English. By eliminating obedience from our thinking, we have slipped into an emasculated form of religion. In our evangelistic activities we have tended to call people to a belief in Jesus but we have failed to tell them that true belief must also involve a willingness to forsake sinful practices and submit to Christ's lordship.

Bonhoeffer saw this clearly when he wrote that belief and obedience must always go together. How can we expect closeness to God if at the same time, we are running away from him? *"Only he who believes is obedient, and only he who is obedient believes."*[18] Such a statement is worth re-reading. The person who disobeys surely does not really believe. Jesus knew this and that may be why he didn't call people to follow a creed. He called us to obey and follow him.

This can give us real hope. When we sense our faith wavering and have trouble believing, what can we do? Obey! Obedience and faith go together, so by bringing our actions into conformity with the Bible's teaching, our faith is rejuvenated.

Books on marriage counseling give a similar formula for handling a loss of love. If your *feeling* of love has grown cold, start doing some loving *actions,* and the feelings will return. As in marriage, so it is in Christianity. When we act differently, changes follow automatically in our feelings and beliefs.

Commitment involves a different view of religion. I have often wondered why the Bible says so little about religion. Jesus strongly criticized the religious leaders in his day because of their arrogance and hypocrisy. Paul, in turn, condemned the "self-made religion" of his contemporaries because it was based on man-made rules. These rules had the appearance of wisdom, but they really were meaningless and of "no value" (Col. 2:21–23). Later, in two brief sentences James warned against worthless religion and gave a concise three-part description of religion which is "pure and undefiled" (James 1:26, 27). Such a description is radically different from the easy believism of our times.

Pure religion involves, first, *a controlled tongue.* Incredible harm can come from words spoken in anger or uttered carelessly. In chapter 3 of his Epistle, James likens the uncontrolled tongue to a roaring fire or an arrow of deadly poison. In contrast, control of the tongue is described as a major mark of personal maturity.

What we say also becomes a mark of spiritual maturity. "If you want to see where a man is spiritually," David Roper has written, "watch him under stress and observe what he says."[19] If a person is truly religious, his or her tongue will be under control and real inner beliefs will be reflected by what is said.

The second mark of pure religion involves *compassionate service to others.* James doesn't mention ostentatious displays of helping which everyone can see and applaud. Instead he writes about visits to distressed widows and orphans.

Mother Teresa received a Nobel Prize for her work among the poor and suffering of Calcutta, but long before she received her check from the King of Sweden, this faithful nun had given herself to service which she never expected anyone to see. If all of our service is visible to others, we will be shallow people indeed.[20] If all of our religion involves ritual and comfortable worship, but doesn't spill over into quiet acts of compassion, we will be a people with very weak religion.

The third characteristic of true religion is a way of *living which is "unstained by the world."* Such a life avoids showing partiality to others, gives freely to the needy, is characterized by good behavior, avoids jealousy and selfish ambition, keeps free of close involvement with secular values, submits to God, develops an attitude of personal humility, treats people fairly, learns to be patient, is nonjudgmental, and avoids complaining.[21] The true believer also is cheerful and involved in prayer and confession. Such a formula is impossible to follow in our own strength but when we submit to the Holy Spirit's control, our values, actions, and personalities all begin to change (Gal. 5:22,23).

I once heard about a Christian leader whose work took him every day through a "red light" district in Chicago. Working in streets dotted with X-rated movie houses, "adult" bookstores, and peep shows, this man was not easily shocked.

One day, however, he saw a sight which distressed him greatly. Coming down the street was a rusted-out Toyota with two large speakers mounted on the front and a large wooden cross tied to the top. The car was painted with religious cliché slogans, and the almost unintelligible preaching sounds coming from the speakers were loud enough to shatter even the noise of the busy street.

"That's religious pornography!" the embarrassed Christian muttered out loud as the car drove by. Its occupants may have been sincere, but they had taken something as wholesome and beautiful as the gospel of Jesus Christ and had cheapened it to compete with the gawdy lights and nude dancers of the inner city.[22]

Perhaps a lot of us have a tendency to cheapen religion. Our intentions may be good, but we make our Christianity into something which matches the gutter mentality of our pagan culture. In contrast, the Bible teaches that religion is worthless if it doesn't commit us to the lofty goals of controlling our speech, helping our neighbors and changing our life styles.

The Cost of Commitment

When I was in high school, our church youth group once went on a retreat where we talked about the issue of persecution. I can still remember my guilt because life seemed so easy and we weren't having any problems because of our faith. I remember, too, the discussion about whether or not Christians should do things that would likely bring about pain and suffering.

Perhaps it is such thinking which leads religious ascetics to live lives of rigorous austerity, self-denial, and masochistic torture. Maybe this is what leads others to talk incessantly about their faith or to drive battered slogan-bearing Toyotas through the streets of Chicago. Such behavior may bring ridicule and persecution but more often this is because of the believer's insensitivity and stupidity than because of his or her faith and commitment.

The Bible never tells us to go out and actively *seek* persecution, but we are instructed to *expect* difficulties to come because of our faith. Corrie ten Boom did not actively look for persecution but surely she was not surprised when the Nazis stormed into her home and arrested her family in response to their quiet acts of compassion. Bonhoeffer's spiritual leadership during the days of Hitler was almost certain to bring the resistance which came. Jesus, Paul and James were consistent in warning that for the Christian, suffering and trials not only are to be expected; they must be accepted joyfully and endured with patience.

Such a conclusion is in stark and radical contrast to the utopian, easy-believist view of Christianity which permeates so much of Christian thinking today. Not all of us suffer like Daniel or the apostle Paul (2 Cor. 11:23–28) and some may live relatively easy lives, but each committed believer must be prepared to face pain, ridicule, criticism, unfair treatment, poverty, family separations, loss of jobs, and even death because of one's faith.

It is difficult for me to both comprehend and to communicate the idea that some day our faith may cost us dearly. We live in a nation which takes pride in tolerating almost any belief. Our nonbelieving neighbors give acceptance and even status to our evangelicalism. Is there a danger that such acceptance will lull us into a complacency which allows no thought about suffering? We live in an affluent society which neither condemns nor ridicules our beliefs, but we are surrounded by a host of nations which, even now, have imprisoned thousands of believers because of their faith. It has been estimated that more Christians have died for their faith in the twentieth century than in all previous centuries combined. If and when such persecution comes to you and me we must not be surprised. Painful persecution is an expected cost of commitment.

Some Conclusions about Commitment

Recently I saw a poster with these words:

GUIDANCE
means that I can count on God;
COMMITMENT
means that God can count on me.

That may be the best definition of commitment that we can find. As we evaluate our own degree of commitment, however, three conclusions are worth pondering.

Commitment must be both personal and public. A hypocrite is a person who really believes one thing but who acts as if he or she believes something else. Such people have also been called dishonest and phony. Many are cowards who are afraid to let their real beliefs be known.

Such phoniness can have no place in the lives of committed believers. If our faith is really sincere, then our inner beliefs must be consistent with our outer behavior. The most stinging condemnation Jesus ever uttered was directed toward those who pretended to be something that they were not. The alternative, however, can be difficult. For you, or me, one of the costs of commitment may be the resistance which comes from others when we really take a stand for what we believe.

In reaching this conclusion, it should be added that on rare occasions, there may be reasons for hiding one's beliefs *temporarily.* For example, Nicodemus and Joseph of Arimathea both kept their beliefs quiet for a while (John 19:38,39), but these were unusual cases and apparently within months after their conversions, each made his beliefs public. The alternative would have been dishonesty and personal insecurity as they tried to live in two conflicting worlds. Much more common and desirable is the example of the disciples who, when they met Jesus, immediately "left everything and followed Him" (Luke 5:11).

Commitment must have both purpose and power. Before there can be total commitment to anything we must see some purpose for our actions and we must know that we have the power to stand firm in our decisions.

What is the *purpose* of commitment? Why should it even concern us? In one sense this whole book is written to answer these questions, but some conclusions are already apparent. A firm commitment gives us a purpose for living and a reason for dying. It helps us to make decisions, to cope with frustrations, and to find meaningful values. Commitment to some purpose removes the emptiness and much of the existential despair from life. It frees us from the trap of "me-first" thinking and motivates us to help others by actions which will make this a better world. For the believer, this Christian commitment brings fulfillment that is lasting and solid because it lets us conform to the Creator's divine plan for human living.

To succeed in maintaining a commitment, however, we need *power*. A costly commitment to Jesus Christ is only possible when we have God's power enabling us to live in God's way. In contrast, easy believism is a lethargic Christianity with no real life or dynamic.

It surely was no coincidence that Jesus talked about power in his final statements before returning to heaven. All the power there is belongs to Christ (Matt. 6:13; 28:18) and he makes it available to his servants (Acts 1:8). Such a conclusion is overwhelming. The committed Christian is no weakling. We Christians have power from on high to do what God wants us to do.

Commitment must be present and periodic. When I got married, I publicly committed myself to my wife. But that was a long time ago. If she never again heard me express my love and devotion, she might begin to wonder if I had changed my mind. Even worse, without periodically reminding myself of this commitment is it possible that I might forget about it too?

Becoming a Christian, I believe, is a once-in-a-lifetime event—just like most of us still get married only once. In contrast, yielding myself to God's will and reminding myself of this commitment is something which should be done often and remembered frequently. If we fail to do this, our commitment tends to become lukewarm and largely meaningless.

When I gave a series of lectures which summarized the contents of this book, a young college student approached me to give his reaction. He had one basic criticism.

"Your ideas on commitment are too strong," he said. "Surely you can't expect modern people to really be fully committed to Christ!"

The Bible gives us no alternative.

We live in a society which values individual rights and personal achievement far more than it appreciates commitment to others. Laziness, greed, fear, self-centeredness, lust, a lack of self-discipline—these have become the guiding principles in this (and perhaps in every) period of history. Such principles are in sharp contrast to the biblical call to commitment and when we see these tendencies in our lives, as we all do at times, they should be attacked one at a time, with the power of the Holy Spirit.

Without commitment, our faith is weak, dull, and about as firm as jelly. It is only with a developing commitment, one which may be costly, that we can begin to move away from the emptiness of easy believism.

Always *being* ready to make a defense
to every one who asks you to give an
account of the hope that is in you, yet
with gentleness and reverence.
1 Peter 3:15

3

Solid Intellectualism

G. Stanley Hall must have been a fascinating man. Born on a
New England farm in the middle of the last century, Hall went to a
country school and, in spite of his father's opposition, decided to do
something that nobody in their little community had ever done
before: Stanley Hall went to college.

He also went to seminary, studied philosophy in Germany, and
became a professor at Antioch College in Ohio. He taught at Harvard, lectured at a newly formed university named Johns Hopkins,
and spent thirty years as the first president of Clark University in
Worcester, Massachusetts.

College presidents today appear to spend most of their time raising money, managing their academic institutions, and working on
public relations. G. Stanley Hall was different. He taught courses
and established himself as one of the earliest and brightest psychologists in America. He was a creative man and an omnivorous reader
who had the rare ability of assimilating masses of information,
synthesizing his learning into concise summaries, and then, driving
home his resultant conclusions in a book, a lecture, or a classroom
presentation. Often he would develop new interests and try to perpetuate these in a professorship, journal or institution, while his

creative mind rushed on to something else. Hall established the first psychological journal in America and was a founder and first president of the American Psychological Association. It was Hall who introduced psychoanalysis to non-European audiences, and who made a significant impact in the early development of child psychology, educational psychology, and the psychology of religion.[1]

In the 1880s this interesting man introduced another idea which has been a part of our lives ever since. In Boston, G. Stanley Hall was the first North American to design a questionnaire and take a survey.

It would be interesting to know how many surveys have been taken during the past century. Unlike the first questionnaire, many surveys today are well designed, carefully administered, and scientifically analyzed. The planning and use of surveys has become a technical art which social scientists have developed to a high state of accuracy. Those of us who are not specialists in the survey-taking field might be able to design questionnaires, but often we fail to realize how difficult it is both to formulate unbiased questions and to analyze the answers accurately.

I thought of this recently when I received a questionnaire from the editor of a widely read Christian magazine. The letter which accompanied the survey indicated that a lot of people don't know where they stand on pacifism, homosexuality, women's rights, abortion, and other social issues. A questionnaire had been prepared, therefore, to get the opinions of 100 evangelical Christians whose conclusions could then be tallied and reported in the magazine.

In response to this invitation, I wrote a polite letter to the magazine editor explaining that I could not fill out the questionnaire. By sending it to only 100 people, he had a very small number of respondents and the results were likely to be biased because the people who received the questionnaire were all friends of the editor who probably would tend to think as he did. Even the questions were phrased in ways which would have influenced our responses. We were asked, for example, if homosexuals should be barred from teaching in public schools, or if women should be drafted into the army—questions which really cannot be answered with a simple "yes" or "no" response. The question-writer's bias was also apparent both in the way the questions were worded, and in the use of capital letters. "Do you agree with 'theories' of evolution that DENY the biblical account of creation?" One survey has asked,

"Do you approve of the open display of PORNOGRAPHIC materials on newsstands, TV, and movies?" Questions like this are phrased in such a way that the answers can be predicted before the survey is ever put into the mail.

Even if these questions had been more carefully written, however, shouldn't we challenge the idea that moral standards and political issues can be settled decisively by the results of a questionnaire? Isn't there a place in our Christianity for some careful thinking? Could it be that the results of such a survey might lead some readers to accept the survey results blindly without thinking through these issues for themselves?

Within the churches there still are pockets of resistance to any careful thinking about one's faith. Some people, it appears, turn off their minds whenever they encounter religious issues, slip into thinking which isn't very deep or logical, and make blind leaps of faith which often have little biblical or other factual basis. Perhaps it has never occurred to some of these people—many of whom may be very sincere and dedicated—that spiritual growth is always stunted when we don't feed on the facts that are presented in the Bible. Other believers may never have been encouraged to think seriously about their beliefs, and maybe some harbor the fear that too much learning or thinking can be dangerous, possibly plunging us into doubt and even nonbelief. Then there are Christians who keep busy with their religious activities and who have no time or interest in study. Would it be accurate to conclude that all of these believers are characterized by what could be called a *nothink* Christianity?

Only slightly better is *shallowthink*—a tendency to give little thought to what we believe, or why—and a preference for reading articles or books which describe personal experiences but give little real substance or instruction. In this age of busyness and television entertainment it is easy to rely on the opinions of others and to slip into the kind of thinking which Paul observed at Corinth. Many of the believers in that early church were like babies whose understanding of spiritual truth was limited because their minds were not developed enough to digest solid "meaty" ideas (1 Cor. 3:2,3).

In an enlightening little book published several years ago, John Stott observed that anti-intellectualism in the churches has been seen most clearly among three influential groups.[2] Many Catholic and *liturgically oriented Christians* sometimes see their rituals degenerate into "ritualism, that is, into a mere performance in which the ceremony has become an end in itself, a meaningless substitute for intelligent worship."[3] *Politically oriented Christians,* in contrast, are obedient to Christ's commands to combat injustice and minister to the poor, but often such social action moves believers away from a study of biblical doctrines or from an appreciation of scriptural teachings about discipleship. *Charismatic Christians,* the third group, are known and admired for their enthusiasm and love but sometimes they make conclusions about truth based on personal experience. They become like the people whom Paul challenged because they had a zeal for God, which was not backed up by biblical knowledge (Rom. 10:2).

Writing in somewhat formal language, Richard Lovelace has concluded that all theological aberrations come when we rely on "subjective experience divorced from the objective control of reason and the written Word of God." When we turn off our minds hoping to let the Holy Spirit lead, we may seem pious at first, but in the end this "dehumanizes us by turning us into either dependent robots waiting to be programmed by the Spirit's guidance or whimsical enthusiasts blown about by our hunches and emotions." This failure to use the mind overlooks the fact that God has given us an ability to gather information and to make rational decisions. Whenever we detour around reason and bypass careful study of the Scriptures we become uncertain about our values, hesitant about our actions, and unable to plan decisively.[4]

This avoidance of thinking also makes us more susceptible to something known as *groupthink.* This word was first used by a Yale University psychologist named Irving Janis who has had a special interest in history and politics. Janis often wondered why important decisions made by groups of brilliant people at the highest levels of government (and industry) sometimes turned out to be wrong. The answer, Janis concluded, was that people who are involved in a cohesive group, and dedicated to a common purpose, often stifle their personal doubts or creative ideas. Such people don't want to "create dissension" or "rock the boat" by expressing views with which the group would disagree. If you are an "advisor to the President," an "up-and-coming member of the company" or even "a respected member of the church," you don't want to antagonize others, lose favor with your leader, or appear to be uncooperative and reactionary. So, as a good group member, you go along with the majority, suppress personal doubts, and convince yourself that "since everyone else seems to be in agreement, and since these other group members are so capable, then surely I am the one who is wrong." Janis discovered situations in government where several group members harbored doubts, but no one said anything because everyone wanted cohesion and unanimity. These people were victims of groupthink.[5]

I wonder how often this kind of thinking permeates churches and Christian parachurch organizations? Motivated by an admirable desire to be submissive or unified, and sincere in not wanting to be a "troublemaker," many individual Christians suppress their doubts and never express their reservations about church programs or plans for the future. Like all victims of groupthink, these believers come to believe that "if the group, and our leaders think it is right, then surely I am wrong." Some of these leaders and other group members would never accept Janis' suggestion that groupthink can only be avoided if people are encouraged to express their reservations and if some members of the group are given the task of raising questions which challenge the group consensus. After full discussion, it often is clear that the majority opinion is right, but without debate, we are less likely to know—"for sure."

The Bible gives no basis for groupthink, and neither does it give us any reason to avoid thinking. In contrast there is considerable scriptural emphasis on the mind. Jesus used his mind in teaching the Scriptures and debating his critics. The Gospels and the Book of Acts were written to provide a factual record of the life and teachings of Jesus and his followers. Paul's Epistles gave rational guidance to people who were becoming established in the Christian faith. Indeed it could be argued that almost all of the New Testament books were written to show the credibility of the Christian message and to answer questions which had arisen in the minds of both believers and critics.[6]

In contrast, it seems that many modern believers have adopted an easy-believism attitude which isn't much concerned with deep thinking or with the importance of solving difficult questions. Many contemporary Christians have forgotten that God created us as thinking beings: he emphasized this when he chose to communicate in words, expects us to love him with our minds (Matt. 22:37), had changed us and given us the mind of Christ (1 Cor. 2:16), and expects us to study and to grow in knowledge (2 Peter 3:18).[7]

A maturing, growing Christianity recognizes that the mind is important. Using our God-given brains we need to struggle with difficult questions:

What do I believe specifically and why?
Does Christianity really make sense?
Can I trust the Bible?
What if I am wrong?
Will Christianity really make any difference in my life?

Since whole books have been written to answer questions such as these,[8] we will only consider basics in this chapter. The three issues which we will consider are important, however, if we are to mature in the Christian walk and in Christian thinking.

Some People Are Not Intellectuals

There may be many believers who become Christians without thinking much about it. They respond to an emotional presentation of the gospel, put their trust in Jesus Christ, and rarely consider whether or not these beliefs make any sense. Although some Christians may be afraid to ask questions lest this shake their faith, it is probable that for a larger number it never even occurs to them that Christians could be able to explain what they believe or know why (1 Peter 3:15).

It is easy to criticize such nonthinkers, especially if we tend to be thinkers ourselves. It is easy to forget, however, God made each of us different, and just as some people are musical while others are not, so some believers are "intellectuals" while others are much less interested in scholarly issues. Some of us like to read and to ponder ideas in depth, but others may be more action-oriented or interested in doing things with their hands. Have you ever noticed how some people enjoy books while others would much rather listen to speakers? I would much rather read a sermon than listen to one. That makes me different from but no better than my friends who rarely open a book but who enjoy listening to speakers, sometimes on cassette tapes which play whenever the car ignition is turned on.

Psychologist Paul Welter has suggested that human beings respond to the world through four channels: *feeling* (experiencing and expressing emotions); *thinking* (being able to plan and to see cause-effect connections); *choosing* (which involves making decisions, establishing standards, and having the courage or willingness to act); and *doing* (or performing whatever action is desirable or necessary).[9] For any one person these four channels are not equal in influence. Most of us have a "wide" channel or two while the other channels are narrower and less powerful. Figure 3–1, which originally appeared in Welter's book, gives a more detailed picture of these four common approaches to life.

Welter uses this chart to suggest that counselors should approach their counselees in different ways. Feeling people express their problems emotionally and respond to acts of warmth and concern. Thinkers are best reached with intellectual challenges. Choosers must be helped to make decisions, to plan ahead, and to select values, while doers should be encouraged to take action and to "get moving." All of this suggests that while some people respond to intellectual arguments, others do not.

If these differences are true for counseling, they also apply to the ways in which we respond to our religion. There will be differences in how carefully we Christians look for reasons to undergird our faith. C. S. Lewis was an intellectual who never would have responded to a hellfire and brimstone sermon or to a music-dominated TV "special." In contrast, others are reached through their feelings and have little desire to study much about why they believe.

Even with these differences, however, each of us has at least some responsibility to understand the Scriptures so we can handle

Fig. 3-1
LIVING CHANNELS

CHANNEL	PERSON WITH STRONG CHANNEL	PERSON WITH WEAK CHANNEL	FORCES ENCOURAGING THESE CHANNELS
FEELING	Aware of own feelings; able to express them.	Doesn't know how to take own emotional pulse; may come across cold or inhibited.	Families, sharing groups, churches (especially where expression of feelings is fostered); coffee break talk.
THINKING	Analytical; investigative frame of mind.	Unaware; impulsive.	Schools, research institutes, games, e.g., chess.
CHOOSING	Courageous; has a clear value structure.	Indecisive.	Politics, religion, advertising.
DOING	Changes behavior when necessary.	Immobilized by deep feelings.	Work, i.e., factories, offices; recreation.

From Paul Welter, *How to Help a Friend* (Wheaton, Illinois: Tyndale, 1977), p. 89. Used with permission.

the Word of Truth with accuracy (2 Tim. 2:15). Failure to know and understand what we believe is inconsistent with the Bible's teaching. This leads us to our second major conclusion.

Christians Must Think Clearly about Their Faith

Why should we know the Scriptures, be able to think clearly, and comprehend both what and why we believe? There are several answers.

Clear thinking is important for evangelism.

As a college student, I learned that we are most likely to reach accurate conclusions when we carefully gather facts from the world around us, and reach logical conclusions based on these facts. If this is how we learn about the world and about other people, shouldn't we be able to do something similar when we ponder the claims of Jesus Christ? No thinking person makes a commitment to something which doesn't make any sense.

In presenting Christ to nonbelievers, it is good to remember that such people will have a limited understanding of spiritual things (1 Cor. 2:14), but we are not asking them to accept what Freud called "an illusion"; a faith which is built on nonfacts. That would be asking people to believe something foolish and irrational and it would overlook the conclusion that there *is* evidence, a lot of evidence[10] to support the Christian position. When this evidence is evaluated with an open mind it then will be (1) ignored and forgotten, (2) rejected, or (3) accepted as credible. If one accepts the evidence, conversion to Christ often follows.

There are some people, of course, who refuse to examine the evidence. Often these are people who take pride in their open minds and intellectual honesty, but they decide against Christianity without even looking at the data. Such people are to be pitied—and prayed for—because they would rather remain in their secularism even if this means that they remain in error. Others look at the data and explain it away so completely that it cannot possibly be examined with objectivity.

In our evangelistic outreach, especially to thinking people, we must learn to research our arguments with accuracy and to present our facts clearly. In reaching these people nothing harms the gospel more than shoddy scholarship, incorrect facts, and conclusions which are not presented clearly and logically. Evangelism, therefore, demands clear thinking. We cannot turn off our brains and still respond in obedience to the Great Commission (Matt. 28:19,20).

Clear thinking strengthens our own faith. In response to an article which I had published in a Christian magazine, a stranger recently wrote an interesting letter. He expressed amazement that a psychologist could be a believer, informed me that there is no evidence to support biblical teaching and stated his conclusion that "in the light of scientific studies, all mysticism, all miracles, all thoughts about the supernatural are wholly mythical." The letter went on to proclaim that no thinking person or "real historian" believes the Bible, and the writer concluded that stories about Jesus are taken "almost word for word" from Hindu literature.

I took the time to respond to this letter in detail. While I respected the writer's freedom to hold convictions which challenged Christian teaching, I was amazed at the sweeping conclusions which he reached without giving any factual data to back up his beliefs. I cited reasons to counteract each of his criticisms and I briefly indicated some of my reasons for believing the biblical record.

A few weeks later my correspondent wrote an eight-page reply which included some legitimate criticisms of born-again Christians who "divide their minds into compartments being critical and rational in matters of science but credulous as children when it comes to religion." Then after citing a host of atheistic writers, the letter concluded that believers engage in "endless propaganda" and are unwilling to accept the evidence against Christianity. "I have a real lack of understanding," the man wrote, "how people of high intelligence can think so clearly on many subjects but when it comes to religion they forget their powers of analysis, their logic and often their common sense."

I did not answer the second letter.

Perhaps I should have challenged some of the writer's biases, acknowledged that I had read some of the atheistic works which he mentioned, and suggested that nonbelievers also ignore data and divide their minds into compartments. Again I could have gently presented the gospel and urged him to consider it seriously. I wondered, however, if writing again would be an exercise in futility.

Christians and nonbelievers alike tend to read what supports their beliefs and biases while overlooking the opinions of those who offer other views. Probably there is no such thing as complete neutrality or nonbias in anyone. Most of us emphasize the facts and ideas which support our beliefs and we tend to ignore or explain away the rest.

The Christian, however, must seek to avoid this kind of bias. The Scriptures indicate that atheists cannot comprehend scriptural truth and are likely to regard the gospel as foolishness (1 Cor. 2:14). That does not give us an excuse for ignoring the nonbeliever and his or her arguments, although it does help us to understand why attempts at communication sometimes seem to accomplish so little.

Many nonbelievers advocate the secular humanism which was mentioned in chapter 1. This is a person-centered system of belief which seeks to help people find meaning in life without resorting to religion. The secular humanist has no tolerance for the concept of sin, has no willingness to believe in God, and tends to see the world as a place where things can and will get better than they are now.

But things aren't getting better and the secular humanist can give no answers to the great questions in life: Who am I? Why am I here? What should I be doing during my time on earth? What happens after death? If taken seriously, atheistic humanism leaves us with despair, emptiness, and hopelessness. There are no firm guidelines for deciding what is right or wrong and, for many, life has no freedom or dignity.[11]

I agree with the conclusion of J. I. Packer who has argued that only the Christian can be a humanist in the fullest sense of the word. Only the believer can rise to become the complete and fulfilled human being that God intended. We may respect the serious thinking of nonbelievers who think that the term "humanism" can only apply to atheists, but we must also agree that "anyone who turns his back on God and God's revealed will for us forfeits a dimension of human dignity and settles for a way of life which in this respect befits the lower animals, but does not match the nature and potential of man at all."[12]

Such a conclusion is sobering and leaves me with a deep sense of thanksgiving. God not only has created us and given us certain freedoms; he also has revealed himself to human beings and enabled millions of people, throughout the centuries, to get at least a limited understanding of his divine ways.

Clear thinking also helps us to know God.
One day several years ago I found myself in prayer, asking to be molded into a man who, throughout life, would become more and more like God. Suddenly an obvious but previously overlooked idea occurred to me. "How can I be like God unless I really understand what God is like?" Soon I was reading books about the nature and attributes of God. This led to a rereading of the Psalms—those Old Testament hymns which perhaps give our clearest picture of what God is like.

It is true, of course, that to understand and to know what God is like does not mean that I will know him personally. Newspaper reports have enabled me to know a lot about current political leaders, but I have never met a politician or head of state so I don't know any of the people personally. I can only know God by meeting with him regularly in times of prayer or meditation, and by having my understanding illuminated by the Holy Spirit. Nevertheless, as I learn more about God with my mind, the better I can know what he is like and the more I can grow into the Christlikeness which he desires.

Clark Pinnock's words are thought-provoking at this point:

> The majority of people do not believe in the gospel because they have a mistaken impression about who God is. Why should they believe in a God they see to be remote, arbitrary, unemotional, strict, sexist, and so forth? Why would anyone expect them to be impressed with intellectual arguments for the existence of such a God, much less feel any desire to love, worship or serve him? Misunderstanding the nature of God is the greatest all time hindrance to becoming a Christian, and understanding him correctly the greatest incentive.[13]

Even a practical New Testament writer like the apostle James gives us a lot of understanding about God's nature. God is wise and willing to share his wisdom (James 1:5); concerned about our present and future lives (1:12); the giver of good and perfect gifts; stable (1:17); righteous (1:20); compassionate (1:2, 5:11); sensitive (2:5); fair in his evaluations (2:13); willing to be near us (4:8); sovereign (4:15); planning to return to earth (5:8); merciful (5:11); able to answer prayer; able to heal; and forgiving (5:15). By using our minds to read God's Word, we begin to comprehend what the Lord is really like and that is important for our spiritual growth.

Clear thinking helps us deal with doubts.

Probably there are Christians who never doubt, but I suspect these people are rare and, at least in some cases, their faith may be impoverished because they never ask questions. Here again, we see individual differences between the fact-oriented people whom psychologist William James called "tough minded" and the more tender individuals who are sensitive and person-centered but less inclined to ponder issues seriously—or to doubt.

In his wisdom, God has chosen not to reveal everything to us at present. Until we get to heaven, our understanding of the universe must be at least somewhat limited (1 Cor. 13:12; Rom. 11:33), because our finite minds are too small to grasp the greatness of divine ideas. This means, however, that some people will always be frustrated because they can't find all of the answers for their questions. For centuries, people have tried to understand why we suffer, or why God does not stop evil, but complete answers escape us and probably will evade us in the future.

Nevertheless, doubt which involves a sincere desire to find answers can create deeper reflection and lead to further discovery.[14] As we seek for answers we discover what we really do know and this can strengthen us spiritually. As we ask God to make us wise, he generously gives wisdom which enables us to be morally pure, gentle, reasonable, full of mercy and good fruits, unwavering, and free from hypocrisy (James 1:5; 3:18). Wisdom from God influences our actions as well as our minds.

Clear thinking brings stability.

One time when the apostle Paul made an appearance in court, he described his conversion and began to talk about the resurrection of Christ.

Suddenly he was interrupted by a Roman official named Festus.

"Paul," he shouted, "you are out of your mind! Your great learning is driving you mad" (see Acts 26:24).

Clearly this was not an accurate description of Paul's mental state but Festus did express a viewpoint that still persists today: the idea that it is possible to become mildly confused and even mentally deranged when one has too much learning.

It is true, of course, that highly brilliant people sometimes do get caught up in such a flood of creative ideas that eventually they withdraw from reality and enter their own little mental worlds of fantasy. More often, however, instability comes when people try to live in accordance with two conflicting beliefs. The person who tries both to serve God and to hold back is doubleminded. The person who makes a request of God but who, at the same time, questions whether God can provide is as unstable as the surf on a wind-tossed sea (James 1:6–8).

In contrast, stability comes when we sincerely place ourselves at the mercy of God and ask him to give peace, stability, and the deep wisdom that he wants to give.

Not long ago I was feeling pressed by the demands of my work, accompanied by some financial and other tensions. Although I kept this to myself, I began to wonder if I was slipping in my psychological stability and efficiency. In desperation one morning I cried out to God and asked him to give me the sound mind, the emotional equilibrium and the inner peace which he has promised in the Scriptures. Nothing dramatic happened but I continued reading the Bible each morning and within a few days it became clear that my prayer was being answered. I was experiencing a marvelous sense of stability and peace.

My experience may not be like yours, but it can be said with confidence that stability is more likely when we stop being doubleminded and yield completely both to his leading and to the teachings of Scripture.

There Are Reasons to Support Our Christian Beliefs

Clark Pinnock is a theologian whose mind is sharp, whose intellect is brilliant, but whose compassion and ability to communicate are down-to-earth. An expert in theology and a respected scholar, Pinnock has studied and written about apologetics—that fascinating field which studies the evidence in support of the Christian religion.

Recognizing that all people are different, Pinnock has suggested that the evidence can be placed in five "circles" which do not have equal appeal to any one person but which together are exceptionally strong and persuasive.[15] Like a rope with five strands, each of the five bodies of evidence may not be all-powerful when alone, but together they make a strong and impressive cable.

The first circle of evidence is *pragmatic*.[16] It asks if faith really gives life meaning and presents evidence to show that it is almost impossible to live consistently with a creed of atheism. People are more than independent amoral individuals who have no clear purpose for living. We are more than a collection of conditioned responses and biological drives. Some nonbelievers have stated that God is no more than a form of wishful thinking, but it could be argued that it is atheism which denies evidence and believes in an illusion. "After all, one can also desire that God *not* exist so that he might not limit our autonomy or stand in the way of what we are planning to do. Because of our desire to do our own thing, we are often tempted to wish God out of existence."[17] And without God, there is no real meaning in life.

The second circle is *experiential* and studies the validity of religious experience. Prior to publicly debating a Moslem leader on the issue of Christ's crucifixion and resurrection, Christian apologist Josh McDowell studied intensively, prayed for his opponent, and asked God for an opportunity to communicate how Christ had changed his life. "I never take a debate unless I know my opponent's position better than he does," McDowell stated, but then he added a thought-provoking idea: "I am convinced that a man with an argument is always at the mercy of a man with an experience."[18]

As we will see in the next chapter, such experiences can be highly subjective and nonbelievers especially are inclined to dismiss the reality of another person's encounters with God. But isn't it prejudice to decide arbitrarily that a whole body of evidence can't be valid since it has never been experienced by the critic? The psychology of religious experience is an infant field which, as it develops, may help us understand our spiritual feelings. In the meantime, we must recognize that for millions of people personal experience provides firm evidence of the truthfulness of Christianity and the reality of God.

Third, the *cosmic* circle looks to the universe around us to see the handiwork of God. For centuries, people have argued that some divine being must exist to give order, beauty, and design to the universe. Such an argument has been challenged, of course, and replaced with alternative explanations including the theory of direc-tionless evolution. Evolution is still a theory under debate and the scientific data is not giving the support that some of its advocates would like to find. Each of us must look at the world and ask honestly—how did it all happen and what holds this world together? The Bible answers clearly that all of this is the work of God (Heb. 1:1–3).

The fourth circle, the *historical,* examines the details of scriptural events and seeks to determine whether or not they are accurate. Did Jesus really come to earth? Did he die and rise again? Did the Flood really occur? What about all of those Old Testament battles? If the Bible is not accurate historically, how can we trust it in other issues?

An examination of books on apologetics shows that the Bible is an historically accurate document which surely can be trusted. The historical evidence is too massive to be presented here, but it is available to anyone who cares to look.[19]

Circle five is a *corporate* body of evidence. It looks to changed lives, reformed attitudes, and people who help one another. It would be foolish to imply that we Christians always do well here. Church splits and disagreements between believers provide clear evidence of division within the body of Christ.

Nevertheless, if we look at the church over its history we see impressive evidence of social concern—giving to the needy, help-ing the sick, resisting slavery, feeding the hungry, building schools and hospitals, ministering in times of crisis. If easy believism con-tinues to gain influence, such social concern is likely to wane. True Christianity, in contrast, must be committed to following Jesus who, in addition to his preaching ministry, compassionately reached out to help the needy.

Pinnock does not mention a *scientific-deductive* circle, but this could be a sixth body of evidence. Can religious experiences really occur? Can we explain some of the miraculous events in the Bible? Did the star of Bethlehem really exist? This is a fascinating and growing field of study which, in time, must include philosophers and theologians as well as natural and social scientists.

Using our minds to understand Scripture; to look for facts which support or refute our faith; to find evidence in nature and in people which shows God's existence and influence; to better understand God and his ways—these are mental activities which deepen our faith.

The alternative is an intellectual superficiality which sways easily. It is a faith similar to that which Jesus described in the parable of the sower. Lacking firm roots, it withers and dies as soon as it encounters the heat of the day. That's a shallow easy-believism which can only be defeated by clear, solid, Spirit-directed thinking.

Discipline yourself for the purpose of
godliness . . . . in speech, conduct,
love, faith and purity, show yourself an
example of those who believe.
1 Timothy 4:7, 12

Now those who belong to Christ Jesus
have crucified the flesh with its passions and desires . . . . But the fruit of
the Spirit is love, joy, peace, patience,
kindness, goodness, faithfulness, gentleness, self-control . . . .
Galatians 5:22, 23, 24

4

Stable Emotionalism

My wife and I waited with a mixture of enthusiasm and anticipation when one of our daughters recently returned from her first plane
trip all by herself. Bounding into the airport she bubbled with exu-
berance and detailed stories which dominated our conversation both
in the car as we drove home and periodically throughout the days
which followed.

One highlight of the trip had been several visits to a church in
Birmingham, Alabama. The sermon and music apparently hadn't
left a great impression but my daughter was overwhelmed by the
friendliness of the people and the hugging. When she suggested that
our family should leave our present church and look for a congregation that emphasized hugging, I gently pointed out that such overt
expressions of warmth and acceptance are not the only bases for
choosing a church.

It is well known that churches differ in the extent to which feelings are acknowledged and their expression encouraged. While
some churches radiate friendliness and warmth (with or without
hugging), others are unfriendly and emotionally cool. While some
worship services are punctuated by spontaneous clapping, shouting
or other expressions of praise from the congregation, others are

much more formal and seemingly dignified. While some sermons tend to tug at the emotional heartstrings of the congregation, others are more intellectual and nonemotional. When individuals and families look for a church to join, there probably is a concern for the theological persuasion of the pastor and congregation but I suspect that people also are influenced by their own emotions and personalities.

Emotions and the Church

It is interesting to ponder why an individual attends one church and not another. Why do some people prefer large churches—or small; evangelical churches—or liberal; Lutheran churches—or those which call themselves Presbyterian, Methodist, Catholic or Pentecostal? Why do some people like churches which encourage hugging, while others do not?

Probably past experience has something to do with our church selection since many of us choose to worship in places which either are like or better than the churches we attended as children. Proximity is important (most of us don't want to travel long distances to church) and more than we might care to admit, many of us also choose churches based on educational, socio-economic, ethnic, and racial issues. Highly educated people, for example, often do not feel "at home" among believers who have little or no formal education. In addition, we could mention the quality of the music, the nature of the sermons, the attitudes of the people and the beliefs of the church leaders—each can influence the choice of a church, sometimes more, perhaps, than the guidance of the Holy Spirit.

Many of these social, personality and emotional differences also influence the ways in which we think about and worship God. Our attitudes toward feelings can affect the tone of our worship services and the extent to which we grow as individual Christians. Three attitudes are especially harmful to spiritual growth.

First, for some people there is an emphasis on *feelingless Stoicism.* In its modern form, this is the view that human beings should be in rigid control of their feelings, unmoved by grief or joy, and not inclined to even whimper over pain and adversity. This is an approach to life which expects us to remain calm and unmoved in all circumstances. It is a somewhat cold, "maintain-a-stiff-upper-lip" philosophy, which appears to have been much more prevalent a century ago but which still dominates some churches today. Among these believers, tears are viewed as a sign of weakness, anger is seen as a lack of self-control, and grieving indicates self-pity. Depression or any other emotional struggle is criticized as the result of sin or a failure to trust God. "Why are you trying to help people who have emotional struggles?" an angry lady once wrote. "If people commit themselves to God they simply can't be depressed and they won't be anxious." Such is the view of those Christians who conclude that all feelings, but especially unpleasant feelings, are to be squelched, hidden, and denied.

This viewpoint is sad because it tries to sweep away some of the very best parts of life. Suppose we could completely smother feelings. Think of how bland life would be. It is true that there would be no sorrow, lonely feelings and discouragement, but there also would be no joy, delight, excitement or laughter.

The Bible clearly teaches that God has feelings. We see this in the descriptions of his love, wrath, laughter, compassion, and joy. We see it, too, in his Son Jesus Christ who cried, was touched by people's needs, became angry, apparently experienced discouragement, and probably laughed.[1]

When we were created in the divine image, God gave us emotions and allowed us to feel, somewhat like he feels. Each of us, at times, gets discouraged, unhappy, and lonely, but at times we can also be enthusiastic, jubilant, overcome with gratitude, and even surprised by joy.

When we consistently stifle feelings, both psychological and spiritual problems can arise. Psychologists have long recognized that feelings which are ignored and pushed aside, still persist. Like overripe fruit that is hidden in the cupboard out of sight, squelched feelings eventually make their presence known in other ways. Angry slips of the tongue, gnawing depression, insomnia, physical aches and pains—these are only a few of the clues which indicate that something is wrong emotionally.

Strict Stoicism also indicates that something is wrong spiritually. The Bible never even hints that we should ignore our feelings or pretend that they don't exist. Even when our Christianity is orthodox and our theology is based on the Scriptures, the believer's religious experience will be dull and faith will have no vitality if it is devoid of feeling.

In contrast to this denial of feelings, some believers embrace the attitude of *unrestrained emotionalism*. Here are Christians who yield completely to their emotions. Church services, and even private worship, are characterized by shouting, exuberant singing, foot-stamping, arm-waving, crying, and other expressions of excitement. The outsider might see this as an indication of feelings gone wild.

In writing to the church at Corinth, the apostle Paul expressed concern about believers who were so carried away with their enthusiasm that they appeared to be crazy. Even today critics of the church like to build some of their condemnations on examples of uncontrolled emotionalism which appear to cast aside clear thinking, and largely ignore the intellectual bases of belief. While recognizing the richness of feelings, Paul indicated that all things should be done in an orderly manner. Since "God is not a God of confusion" the emphasis in worship services should be on edification and sound teaching (1 Cor. 14:23, 40, 33, 26). Even in church—perhaps especially in church—emotions can be expressed, but they must also be controlled.

A third attitude could be labeled *psychological subjectivism*. Unlike the unrestrained emotionalism which can sweep those people along who rarely give their actions much thought, subjectivism is more subtle. This view is held by those who conclude, sometimes even by rational means, that feelings are a valid guide for behavior. "Be sensitive to your feelings," this modern philosophy proclaims. "Keep 'in touch' with your emotions, accept your feelings and don't be afraid to show them. You don't have to be a closed, insensitive person. Instead, you should admit how you feel, be open to sharing your feelings honestly, and be willing to let emotions guide your actions." "It can't be wrong if it feels so right," a popular song has proclaimed. "If it feels good, do it!"

Such a viewpoint may have begun as a reaction against the stuffy Stoicism of the previous century, but the new "feeling-focused" approach to life has been nurtured and brought to full bloom by postwar American psychology. Concerned about the dangers of suppressed emotion, and influenced by the creative ideas of Freud, influential writers like Carl Rogers and Abraham Maslow began to develop schools of thought which came to be known as part of the self-psychology movement. The emphasis was on being authentic, open, honest, and "self-actualized." Encounter groups and sensitivity sessions became popular forms of therapy and the value of introspection became widely accepted. Television and radio programs carried the new message, and so did newspapers, magazines, and the writers of some self-help books. It is not surprising that this viewpoint also permeated churches and contributed to the easy-believism approach to Christianity.

I would be dishonest if I pretended to be one who opposes all self-psychology. I agree with its premise that emotions become dangerous when they are denied. There *is* value in openness, in self-examination and in honestly speaking the truth, in love.

Like a swinging pendulum, however, the new self-psychology has moved away from an extreme Stoicism, has rejected unrestrained emotionalism and has taken us to a subjectivism which is highly dangerous, especially because it has destructive characteristics which are subtle and difficult to observe.

Psychological subjectivism is dangerous, for example, because it is primarily self-centered. A recent survey reported that seven out of ten Americans "spend a great deal of time thinking about themselves" and those questioned reported that this is a significant change from their previous habits of thought.[2] The survey did not ask what these people think about specifically, but several recent writers have observed that many of us think almost constantly about our own desires, urges, goals, and problems. There is less emphasis on self-sacrifice or self-denial for the good of others but great attention given to "my-ism": my money, my success, my rights, my freedom, my pleasure, my personal growth, my feelings. Can anything be so narrow and ultimately so dull as a life focused almost exclusively on ourselves?

Such self-centered introspectionism leads to another danger—the tendency to ignore sin, overlook the need for repentance, and forget about outside sources of authority. Me-centered people rely on their feelings for deciding what is right or wrong. They tend to abandon scriptural teachings about discipline, morals, commitment, restraint, and ideals, while they elevate feelings—many of them fleeting—to become the measure of what one is supposed to be and how we should act.[3]

All of this is a form of idolatry! God has been replaced by an emphasis on ourselves. Personal feelings have been elevated to a place of authority above the Scripture. In its extreme forms, concern for others is forgotten in the hedonistic drive to satisfy our own lusts and to fulfill our own pleasures.

Within Christian circles, this self-philosophy is expressed in the easy believism which was described in chapter 1. Often the Scriptures no longer control our lives. Outside authority is rejected and replaced by theologies based on personal experience and on the priority of smooth interpersonal relationships. By largely ignoring self-control, such a view allows people to convince themselves that they are free. Few recognize that the person who is controlled by his or her own personal urges and feelings is in the worst kind of bondage. When we are not in control of our emotions, these same emotions control us!

Emotions and Self-Control

Is it possible to admit that we have feelings and to experience the richness of our emotions, without falling into Stoicism, unrestrained emotionalism, or psychological subjectivism? Within recent years, a number of Christian writers have addressed this question[4] and have helped us to understand and to handle feelings—especially troublesome emotions such as anger, depression and anxiety.

The messages in these self-help books are often similar. When troublesome emotions appear, we are encouraged to:

- Admit to ourselves that the feelings are present.
- Communicate with God about the troublesome feelings and find at least one or two trusted friends with whom we can talk.
- With the help of these friends, try to discover what is causing the feelings.
- Ponder what we, as individuals, can do about the causes of these feelings—then do it.

Emotional control rarely comes by deliberately trying to stop feelings. We can try repeatedly to stop anxiety, for example, or to pull ourselves out of depression—but such frontal attacks rarely succeed.

More helpful is a combination of clear thinking (in which we try to determine what is causing the problem and how we might think more positively or more realistically), changed behavior (in which we clear our lives of sinful or unproductive actions and determine to act differently) and obedience to the guidelines of Scripture. Since self-control is listed as one of the fruits of the Spirit (Gal. 5:23), we can expect that, in time, such control will come when we yield ourselves regularly to the Holy Spirit's control.

The Bible's emphasis on self-control (Titus 1:8; 2 Peter 1:6) does not imply that troublesome or painful feelings will never be present in the believer. To be human is to experience emotion. This includes joy and love, but it also involves discouragement, anger, and sorrow which is not likely to be gone completely until we get to heaven (Rev. 21:4). In the Garden of Gethsemane, Jesus was in control of his emotions, but he still felt anguish and depression. He didn't "fall apart" at the grave of Lazarus, but he still grieved and wept. He wasn't giddy or silly with delight when the disciples showed their ability to minister, but he was clearly pleased (Luke 10:17–24).

When he wrote to the suffering Christians, James didn't tell the readers to hope that their feelings would go away. He encouraged them, talked about joy, and then let them know that they could learn to endure pain and grow because of the unhappy events in their lives.

As Christians, we need to face our feelings and learn self-control, but it should never be our goal to have an emotion-free Christianity.

Emotions and the Christian

Psychologists have always had difficulty studying emotions because feelings change whenever we start analyzing them. When the psychologist starts looking at the angry, anxious or depressed person, for example, these emotions tend to get worse, decline, or become mixed with other feelings. When we get to emotions like joy, peace or awe, the psychologist is even more stymied, first because these emotions seem so rare in our world, and second because these feelings don't arouse us to a state that can easily be seen by others or described in words.[5]

It may be helpful to think of emotions as existing in three parts.[6] The *conscious* part refers to what we feel and can report to others. Anger, jealousy, contentment, shame, disgust, and excitement are examples of conscious feelings which most of us experience at times. This probably is what comes first to mind when we think about emotion.

There is, however, a *behavioral* part of emotion. At times we smile, scowl, cry, clap our hands, giggle, jump for joy, laugh, or run in fear. All of these are learned reactions and each can indicate the presence of emotion.

Underneath are the *physiological* responses which can't always be seen or felt, but which indicate that emotion is present. Examples include increases in blood pressure and rate of heartbeat, the standing up of hair to cause "goose pimples" on the skin, secretions of various glands and the draining of blood from the stomach tissues which sometimes causes what we call "butterflies."

For almost a century scientists have debated and experimented to find which of these three—conscious, behavioral or physiological—comes first and triggers the others. The technical theories and discussions about this need not concern us here. It is enough to recognize that all three parts of emotion exist and make their appearance in time. Sometimes, for example, we may feel depressed, and our body reflects this physiologically—but we can hide our feelings from others so they never suspect our inner turmoil. At other times the body "knows" there is stress and tension. We don't recognize this consciously or show this in our actions until we discover the presence of an ulcer or high blood pressure—which are two of the body's ways of crying "ouch." On rarer occasions it may be that we can feel and act out our feelings, but there is little inner physiological change.

When we commit our emotions to God, can we expect him to influence all three parts—our conscious feelings, our outward actions, and our inner physiology? I believe that the answer is a clear "yes."

Instead of rejecting, denying, or yielding to emotion, we need to submit these emotions to divine control. The growing Christian is grateful for his or her feelings. We are grateful for the love, peace, joy, and contentment which only God gives. And we are determined to learn from the hatred, anger, jealousy, and sorrow, even though we hope to see these reduced and in some cases banished completely from our lives.

We must avoid the attitude which treats emotions as "second class citizens"[7]—a part of life which is tolerated but clearly of less importance than faith or theological understanding. God is the creator of feelings; his Holy Spirit enables us to enjoy and grow through our emotions (Gal. 5:22–25).

Emotions and Self-Fulfillment

Once, in every three or four years, some perceptive writer produces an in-depth book which analyzes the current state of the culture and stimulates a lot of thinking and discussion.[8] Only time will tell if Daniel Yankelovich has written such a volume but his *New Rules in American Life: Searching for Self-Fulfillment in a World Turned Upside Down*[9] is a sobering analysis of our present society.

Based on mountains of research statistics, the book presents the view that we are moving into a cultural revolution which will transform morals and our whole way of living. Old values such as hard work, faithfulness to one's mate, or dedication to one's children are being thrown away. Instead of the "self-denial ethic" which once ruled our lives, "we now find people who refuse to deny themselves *anything*—not out of bottomless appetite, but on the strange moral principle that 'I have a duty to myself.'"[10]

According to Yankelovich, this new revolution has come out of two trends in North American society: a psychology which has emphasized self-fulfillment, and an economy which has made such fulfillment possible. Both the psychology and the economy are now changing, however, and people are finding themselves in a three-part bind which has real emotional implications.

The first bind comes because of our desire for freedom and self-fulfillment. This desire is so powerful that many of us are unwilling and unable to make choices about values, careers, and beliefs. Although presented with an abundance of choices, some people "value their personal freedom so intensely that they regard each new choice and commitment demanded of them as a threat to their freedom and a challenge to the other possibilities"[11] which might arise. Because they are reluctant to commit themselves to anything—"for sure"—many people live lives which are continually changing and emotionally unsettled.

The frustration of this viewpoint can be overwhelming. Think, for example, of the couple who believes that self-fulfillment comes only when they have a career, marriage, children, freedom, independence, security, money, simplicity, gracious living, time to read, and friends. Many of these clearly conflict, but a generation of people still clings to the belief that fulfillment only comes when *all* of their desires are met.

This could be ignored if the description were fantasy, the pipe dream of some social psychologist or philosopher who was merely speculating. But this picture of modern human beings is based on careful research and I am left with the uncomfortable conclusion that this describes many Christians. We tell ourselves and each other that true fulfillment is found only in Christ. We admire Paul who wrote about his ability to be content regardless of the circumstances (Phil. 4:11). Then we leave church or get up from our knees and join the world as it searches for fulfillment by striving for goals which sometimes conflict: dedication to the family, dedication to church and dedication to career; hard work which earns money versus leisure time which gives rest; laying up treasures in heaven versus the storing of treasures on earth; having freedom to be independent or creative as opposed to becoming a successful member of some academic or business organization.

A second bind arises because we value independence but recognize that self-fulfillment only comes when there is cooperation with others. Many of our plans include career advancement, flexible work arrangements, low-cost travel, opportunities for creativity and sometimes acclaim and acceptance—all of which involve other people. Furthermore, we are beginning to discover that the economy, which is dominated by other people, may not allow such freedom. Prices and interest rates are high, jobs may be scarce, transportation is expensive, and saving seems impossible. All of this hinders our dreams and blocks our goals. Slowly we are coming to see what Jesus taught centuries ago—we cannot live in isolation, dreaming dreams but ignoring God and our fellow human beings.

Perhaps this clash between self-fulfillment and our relationships with others comes into greatest clarity over the issue of intimacy. Introspection and a feeling-dominated life style pull us away from people and bring both loneliness and depression. Intimacy and closeness, however, require that we spend time with others and this hinders our desire to be independent. Erich Fromm outlined this problem many years ago. We are torn, he said, between the needs to be related and rooted in others, and the need to transcend our animal nature in order to find identity[12] and creative fulfillment.

Third, it appears that many people are caught in a constant preoccupation with their inner psychological needs. They work on the assumption that emotional cravings are sacred objects—rigid needs which *must* be satisfied. Such thinking assumes that it is a crime against nature to harbor an unfulfilled need. But other people have needs, too, and these sometimes conflict with mine. We already have seen that some "needs" simply cannot be met, and this realization leaves us frustrated, unfulfilled, and sometimes angry.

Yankelovich's perceptive analysis is not written from a Christian perspective but his conclusions begin to sound very biblical. Apparently without realizing that this idea came from Jesus, Yankelovich concludes that any serious seeker of self-fulfillment must grasp the truth that "to find one's self one must lose oneself." To be free of the emotional binds which come from self-psychology, we must make commitments that endure over time. We must be willing to make decisions about our beliefs, our priorities, and our willingness to be involved with other people.

The alternative is to continue floundering emotionally as well as spiritually as society's values change and economic realities limit our freedom. We cannot remain comfortably entrenched in the easy believism philosophy. We must move away from self-absorption and toward a greater commitment to God and to other people. Perhaps in time we will begin to see new meaning in the words of James who wrote that an emphasis on pleasure and self-fulfillment is the source of quarrels, conflicts, lust, frustration and even murder (James 4:1–3).

Our lives on earth can be fulfilled and emotionally rich, but we must never forget that until we get to heaven, each of us is "like a vapor that appears for a little while and then vanishes away." Our responsibility, therefore, is not to be running after fulfillment. We find fulfillment when we are determined to know what is right, and to do it! (James 4:14, 17).

Emotions and Moral Pain

Even when there is a sincere desire to know God's truth, and to obey it, some people never reach the goals of personal fulfillment and freedom from inner emotional turmoil.

Following the truce in Viet Nam, thousands of American servicemen returned home, only to discover that the country was still in turmoil over the morality of the war. There were few bands or parades to welcome back the men and women who had served in Southeast Asia. Many veterans, including those who had sustained life-changing injuries, encountered scorn, criticism, and even rejection in exchange for their dedication and personal sacrifices overseas.

But life had to go on so the veterans looked for jobs and started building careers and families. For a while, the country tried to forget Viet Nam, but after several years it was becoming clear that many of the veterans were falling apart psychologically. Nightmares, uncontrollable outbursts of anger, anxiety, intense feelings of quiet depression—the symptoms were the same and some psychiatrists began to talk of a "delayed stress syndrome" which had remained hidden during the post-Viet Nam years.

Then a writer named Peter Marin expressed another opinion. He concluded that psychological stress was not the real problem. Instead, the veterans were suffering from a deeply cutting moral pain. As a society, Marin suggested, we don't know how to approach guilt or moral dilemmas. The language and techniques of psychology are powerless to deal with the shame or the deep moral distress which gets imbedded in people who have murdered and maimed because they were told to do so.

There was little sense of patriotism or pride in their sacrifices. Instead, the veterans were becoming increasingly aware of inner feelings of guilt over their actions in the war. Many were still pondering the suffering, the contrast between Asian poverty and American affluence, the seeming stupidity of the killing, and the fact that they had seen the real horror of war. Some felt that they had been "used" by the politicians, and many were unable to trust or love. They returned then to a society which, Marin suggests, doesn't know how to approach guilt or moral dilemmas.

> Our great therapeutic dream in America is that the past is escapable, that suffering can be avoided, that happiness is always possible, and that insight inevitably leads to joy. But life's lessons . . . teach us something else . . . the world is real; the suffering of others is real; one's actions can sometimes irrevocably determine the destiny of others; the mistakes one makes are often transmuted directly into others' pain; there is sometimes no way to undo that pain—the dead remain dead, the maimed are forever maimed, and there is no way to deny one's responsibility or culpability, for those mistakes are written, forever and as if in fire, in others' flesh.[13]

What Marin has written about veterans applies equally to all of us. With the passage of time, the reality of our moral struggles can no longer be hidden. When the truth about past actions becomes apparent, the morally distressed almost always become more troubled—psychologically and spiritually.

Taking their cues from the proven methods of psychology and psychiatry, Christian counselors have encouraged believers to deal with their emotional turmoil and moral pain by expressing feelings and talking about life's past events. But even after such talking, the pain often persists and the emotionally distraught fail to get better. Secular voices talk weakly about the need for every human being to find meaning in life and freedom from guilt, but these voices also talk of futility, hopelessness, and the realization that our modern humanistic culture has no answer to the moral pain lodged in the hearts of so many individuals.

Admitting the existence of such emotional turmoil is a healthy first step toward a solution. When guilt and shame are denied or squelched, there can be no healing and no experience of inner peace. Facing guilt and moral pain honestly and discussing these with a compassionate friend or counselor can be an important step toward emotional freedom.

Real and lasting release does not come, however, until we confess our sins to God and pour out our hurts, talking like David so often did in the Psalms. When we confess our sins, God forgives completely and cleanses us within (1 John 1:9).

There are times, however, when we may know that God forgives, but since we don't feel forgiven—the moral pain persists. Does the Bible offer any escape from this emotional bind? To answer, let us ponder three meetings between Jesus and some distraught people.

In Mark 9, we read of an incident where a large crowd had gathered around the disciples, the local religious leaders, and a young boy who was "possessed by a spirit" and repeatedly convulsed by epileptic-type seizures. No one knew how to help the boy until Jesus came and brought both instant healing and inner peace.

In the midst of this real-life drama, the boy's father was asked if he believed that Jesus could bring healing. "I do believe," the father replied, but with refreshing honesty he added, "help me overcome my unbelief!" (Mark 9:24, NIV).

Could this short prayer be a model for people who suffer emotional and moral pain? "Lord, I believe; help me to overcome my unbelief" and my tendencies to doubt that I am forgiven. When we need cleansing we must confess our sins, ask for divine forgiveness and then pray that God will give us the inner conviction that forgiveness has really occurred.

On another occasion Jesus came upon a group of people who had caught a woman committing adultery and were preparing to stone her. In reading of this incident, we can almost sense a self-righteous and sadistic glee in the religious leaders as they prepared to punish the woman. It is unlikely that they appreciated the observation of Jesus that the first stone should be hurled by the person who was without sin.

Slowly, perhaps sheepishly, the accusers walked away until Jesus and the woman were alone. She knew that he had forgiven her, but she also was given some practical advice: "Go your way and sin no more."

Confession doesn't mean much and a sense of forgiveness doesn't come if we choose to keep on sinning. God knows that we sin repeatedly and he is willing to forgive again and again. Nevertheless, he wants us to have a determination to avoid both mental and behavioral immorality. In our own strength, we are powerless to resist temptations, but God has promised to help. He enables us to live lives which are more pure and honoring to him (1 Cor. 10:13). Like the woman caught in adultery he helps us to go on our way through life and "sin no more."

This must have been the desire of Zacchaeus—that little tax collector who had climbed into a sycamore tree so he could get a better view as Jesus walked by. When the Lord spoke to Zacchaeus, and forgave his cheating, the tax man's response was dramatic.

"Look Lord!" he exclaimed (Luke 19:8). "Here and now I give half of my possessions to the poor, and if I have cheated anybody out of anything, I will pay back four times the amount" (NIV). Zacchaeus didn't have to do anything to pay for Christ's forgiveness. That forgiveness comes as a divine gift to anyone who asks. But often we feel better when our confession is followed by actions which help others. Zacchaeus determined to make restitution to those whom he had hurt, but he didn't stop there. He also promised to help the poor.

Sometimes it is impossible to undo what we have done in the past. Like those Viet Nam veterans, we cannot go back to raise the dead or heal those who have been physically, psychologically, or spiritually maimed by our past actions, sins or moral failures.

We can experience emotional cleansing, however—by honestly

facing and admitting our sins; by confessing our faults to God and to one or two compassionate believers (James 5:16); by asking God to help us really believe and accept the fact that we are forgiven; by seeking to live a life that resists sin; and by reaching out in acts of compassion to people who are in need.

Psychologists have long been impressed by the conclusions of a Jewish theologian named Martin Buber who proclaimed the importance of "I-thou" relationships in which two people show mutual respect and care for one another. In writing about veterans, Marin[14] has proposed that we must think in terms of "I-thou-they"—a way of thinking which recognizes the importance of other people in addition to the counselor and counselee. We who are believers are members of the body of Christ and residents in a larger society. Our responsibilities extend to other people and it is from others that we receive acceptance, encouragement, and support.

Many people have discovered, however, that the intimacy of a counseling relationship and the support of a social group still are unable to completely eradicate emotional and moral pain. In addition there must be divine help and forgiveness. Real healing comes only when we have an "I-thou-they-Him" relationship. Without him, our moral pain persists; it is only with his help and forgiveness that emotional turmoil is permanently resolved and removed.

In my early days as a Christian I conformed to the old masculine view of feelings: men don't cry, don't get excited, don't show too much love. As I read more about God, however, and studied the life of Jesus—our model—I began to see a full range of emotions. Envy and vindictiveness were not there, but love, sensitivity, and peace shone forth in abundance. At times, too, there was anger over injustice and hatred of sin mixed in with sorrow and deep compassion. There was an understanding of moral pain and a concern about emotional turmoil.

It must be of significance that the fruits of the Spirit (Gal. 5:22, 23) almost all describe emotional states which God wants in the life of believers. He wants us to show a tender, sensitive, honest and controlled emotionalism. This is an emotionalism which admits guilt and sincerely seeks divine help in overcoming emotional and moral pain. This emotionalism leads to a balanced perspective on our feelings and that, surely, is a mark of maturing Christianity.

You are not of the world.

John 15:19

Don't let the world squeeze you into its
own mold. . . .

Romans 12:2 (Phillips)

This is pure and undefiled religion in
the sight of our God and Father, to visit
orphans and widows in their distress,
and to keep oneself unstained by the
world.

James 1:27

5

A Separated Life Style

The history of the world is a long chronicle of nations and individuals dominating one another and striving to be free of dom-
ination. For centuries, while political rulers have taken delight in
conquering nations, oppressed peoples have struggled to cast off the
chains of authority. These struggles are invariably verbal, sometimes violent and often both, but on rare occasions a leader rises
who advocates nonviolent resistance instead of war and fighting.
Martin Luther King was such a leader and so was Mohandas Ka-
ramchand Gandhi.

The people of India called Gandhi the Mahatma, or Great Soul. A
serious and somewhat shy man who spent his life searching for
truth, Gandhi lived a simple life style dominated by self-denial and
a tolerant concern for others. He was so deeply distressed by the
social injustice his people suffered under colonial rule that he developed a new method for bringing social change. The method involved courage, nonviolence and a belief that the way in which a
person acts is more important than what he or she achieves. Gandhi
achieved a great deal before his assassination at age 78. He helped
lead his country to independence and he inspired millions with his
example and teachings. When asked by a reporter to summarize his

beliefs, Gandhi did not give a lengthy theological discourse. He replied simply, "My life is my message."

It has been reported that Gandhi, a Hindu, was deeply impressed by the Sermon on the Mount and read it frequently. He might have agreed with a famous British preacher who wrote: "If you want to have power in your life, go straight to the Sermon on the Mount. Live and practice it and give yourself to it"[1]; then expect your life to change.

The change will not be in the direction of easy believism. Another British preacher, John R. W. Stott, has argued that the Sermon on the Mount gives a description of what Jesus wants his followers to be and to do.

> The followers of Jesus are to be different—different from both the nominal church and the secular world, different from both the religious and the irreligious. . . . Here is a Christian value system, ethical system, religious devotion, attitude to money, ambition, life-style and network of relationships—all of which are totally at variance with those of the non-Christian world.[2]

During a Bible study which my wife and I attended, one of the participants made a startling statement after we had begun to study the Sermon on the Mount.

"Nobody can live like that!" my friend exclaimed.

The speaker was a dedicated Christian and a successful businessman, but he was honest enough to admit that the teachings of Jesus seem impossible to apply in our modern era. Some theologians have concluded that the sermon's teachings are so optimistic and unrealistic that nobody could obey them. It hardly seems possible, however, that Jesus would have presented a goal if he knew it was an unattainable ideal which we could ponder intellectually but never apply personally. He implied that this was a divine standard toward which each Christian should strive. To take the sermon seriously, however, is to bring a life style which could make us at least as different from others as Gandhi was from his contemporaries.

Jesus and the Christian Life Style

Gandhi was not the first man who tried to live in accordance with his beliefs. For centuries, dedicated people have striven to bring their beliefs and their behavior into conformity, but only Jesus was able to reach this goal with perfection. His whole life style was a reflection of the teaching which he gave in the Sermon on the Mount.

It would be impossible to select a core portion of the sermon which summarized the rest. In terms of life style, however, no words are more decisive than the following:

> You are the salt of the earth; but if the salt has become tasteless, how will it be made salty again? It is good for nothing any more, except to be thrown out and trampled underfoot by men.
> You are the light of the world. A city set on a hill cannot be hidden. Nor do men light a lamp, and put it under a peck measure, but on the lampstand; and it gives light to all who are in the house.
> Let your light shine before men in such a way that they may see your good works, and glorify your Father who is in heaven.
> (Matt. 5:13–16)

This is the part of Jesus' sermon which caused my friend in the Bible study to balk. I can understand his frustration because the examples of salt and light present us with a powerful challenge. Jesus doesn't state here what we should be, will be, or can become. He states that we *are* salt and light.

In considering this, let us ponder *the penetrating power of salt.* In the time of Jesus, salt was highly valued for two reasons: it kept things from going bad in a time when there was no refrigeration, and it added flavor.

To conclude that our world is getting better and better would require not only incredible optimism, but total disregard of the overwhelming evidence. In Romans 1, Paul gives a grim description of a world without God, and it doesn't take much imagination to realize that this picture looks like the front pages of our newspapers today.

Living in this kind of an environment, Christians are expected to be like a "moral disinfectant" which God uses to stop decay "in a world where moral standards are low, constantly changing, or nonexistent."[3] To have such a preservative influence, we must be in contact with the world, just like the salt is rubbed into the meat, but we must keep some separation from secular influences.

It has been shown scientifically that salt in itself never loses its saltiness or power to prevent decay. In Bible times, however, there were no refineries so salt often got mixed in with impurities which rendered it useless—except to be used as road dust. It still looked like salt but it didn't act like salt.[4] The same can be true of modern believers. If we get mixed up with the impurities of this world our penetrating power will be gone. If we don't want to appear different from others, or if we refuse to challenge the evil and dishonesty around us, our influence will be minimal.

For Christians there always is the possibility that we will become like salt which sits by itself in a fancy salt shaker but never is used to preserve or to add flavor. People around us live blah and meaningless lives. If we don't penetrate the society they will never see that only Christ adds a savory radiance to life.

It is not easy to improve society and neither is this goal likely to make us popular. But Jesus gives us no choice. We have a responsibility to condemn evil and to stop social decay as best we can. That must be a part of the Christian life style.

Then we must also radiate the *illuminating power of light.* Life for the Christian is more than a constant condemning of evil. We have the privilege, in addition, of spreading light in this dark world.

Salt is able to do its work without being seen, but light must be visible and then it can accomplish three purposes.[5]

• Light clears away darkness. Jesus described himself as the light of the world who came to remove the darkness caused by human sin and ignorance. Just as the moon reflects light from the sun and brightens the darkened sky, so we must get our energy from the Son of God and shine as lights before other people. We do this by living a life style which is "good" and which clearly points people to God (Matt. 5:16).

• Light also guides and shows us where to go. Sometimes, when driving along a lonely road at night I will slow down to a crawl and turn off the headlights for a few minutes. The sensation is eerie and could lead to a fearful frustration—except for the fact that I can always pull the switch and turn on the lights again.

My psychology books and my contacts with people tell me that a lot of us are like the driver in the dark without the headlights. Is it too simplistic to say that many Christians know the source of light—Jesus Christ—but we would rather let people stay in the dark and even flounder ourselves because we don't want to be seen with the light?

• Light warns of danger. Jesus implied this when he talked one night to a powerful religious leader. Some people prefer to stay in darkness, Jesus said, because light will show up their evil deeds.

That can be both embarrassing and uncomfortable (John 3:19–21). It can also be threatening to see our self-centered deeds in a new light, and be forced to face the implications of our actions.

True disciples of Jesus Christ do not try to hide in the world and obliterate any differences between us and our non-Christian friends and neighbors. Of course we want to be sensitive to others and to respect their viewpoints, but we also must accept the responsibility of resisting evil; standing boldly for what is true and right; working to strengthen our homes and to improve our societies (since God has established these institutions to curb sinful influences in the world)[6]; and doing ''good works'' which are designed to point people to God rather than to boost our own egos. Perhaps you may want to re-read the previous sentence and ponder how it can apply to your attitudes, your world, your school, your neighborhood, even your church. Such thinking is an important step in the direction of finding a realistic Christian life style.

Rules and the Christian Life Style

Fundamentalism, according to one dictionary definition, is a movement within American Protestantism which believes that the Bible is without error, not only in matters of faith and morals but in its recording of historical facts. The term first came into prominence following the first world war when liberal trends in theology were becoming widely popular and more conservative Christians felt a need to defend the historic fundamentals of their faith. According to theologian James Packer[7], the early fundamentalists defended such issues as the inspiration, authority and infallibility of Scripture; the deity of Christ; his virgin birth and miracles; his atoning death for our sins; the importance of evangelism and salvation by faith in Christ; and the power of prayer.

As a summary of theological beliefs, fundamentalism is still widely accepted but many who agree with the theology shun the fundamentalist label. ''Fundamentalism'' is a term which now seems to apply less to historic Christian theology and more to a group of people who are known best for their restrictive practices and conservative political views. The lists of criticisms differ, but most frequently fundamentalists have been chided for their intellectual rigidity, intolerance of views which differ from their own attitude of spiritual superiority, eccentric individualism, exclusivism, indifference to churchmanship, and controversial involvement in social issues.

Most religious observers probably would agree that the old Fundamentalist-Liberal controversy has died but most of us who believe in the orthodox fundamentals of the faith prefer to be known as "evangelicals" or simply "Christians." The fear of scholarship has gone, a sincere concern about social injustice has developed, there is a greater willingness to cooperate with others of like precious faith, and many Christians who accept the authority of Scripture have shifted from a defensive to an offensive stance. While retaining the theological basics of the old fundamentalism, we have attempted to cast off the practices, suspicions, and narrow-minded attitudes which brought fundamentalism into disrepute.

Nowhere is this shift away from fundamentalism seen more clearly than in our struggles with life style. Two or three decades ago, the fundamentalist subculture provided us with a list of rules. These differed from one location to another, but in general "real Christians" were expected to show their uniqueness by not smoking, drinking, dancing, attending movies or missing church. Sometimes involvement in politics or in academics was added to the list of prohibited activities and the "social gospel"—which involved a compassionate caring for the needy—was condemned because it seemed to be the major mark of theological liberalism.

These rules were not always stated explicitly, but they were clearly known by the insiders, and enforced by the unmentioned but subtle threat of social ostracism. Many of us who grew up in such circumstances were made to feel guilty if we broke the rules. Probably many of us felt that we were missing out on the "real fun" because of these prohibitions, but we did have clear guidelines and undoubtedly were kept from many painful and sinful experiences because of the rules.

Deep within the nature of human beings, however, there seems to be an urge to break rules whenever they appear. In addition, evangelical Christians have come to see that many of the old rules were rigid, and more a reflection of tradition than an evidence of careful Bible study. Slowly, therefore, a shift has taken us away from a rule-dominated life style. In many respects this is good, but the shifts also have involved us in making more and more compromises with the larger culture in which we live.

Richard Quebedeaux has summarized this with great clarity.

> The influence of the wider culture on the contemporary evangelical movement has been nothing less than staggering. . . .
> It took a long time for the evangelicals to really break away from the (largely working-class) cultural ghetto of fundamentalism and join the ranks of mainstream society. Quite frankly, the basic theology and behavior of fundamentalists and evangelicals remained very similar. . . .
> Evangelicals decided to enter the world to change it—a world that could no longer take the message and lifestyle of fundamentalism seriously, if it ever did in the past. They began to affirm the Christ who transforms culture. The evangelicals knew that to influence the world for Christ they would have to gain its attention in a positive way. In a word, they would have to become respectable by the world's standards. . . .
> In the course of establishing their respectability in the eyes of the wider society, the evangelicals have become harder and harder to distinguish from other people. Upward social mobility has made the old revivalistic taboos dysfunctional. Evangelical business people, professionals, clergy, and students began traveling the world and soon discovered born-again believers in Europe, Africa, and Asia who drink and smoke—something American evangelicals had been told since childhood was wrong. They changed their minds. Furthermore, evangelical business people, professionals, and celebrities gradually found it necessary (and pleasant) to travel the cocktail-party circuit in Beverly Hills, San Marino, San Francisco, Dallas, Scarsdale, and Washington, D.C., and the cocktails became increasingly difficult to refuse. Evangelical young people learned how to dance and openly "grooved" on rock music. Professors in evangelical colleges and seminaries took up pipe smoking just like their liberal and secular colleagues. And evangelical magazines and newspapers began reviewing plays and movies.[8]

In this scramble to move away from the old fundamentalism so that we could gain respectability with the world, many evangelicals went from one extreme to the other and developed what might be called a new fundamentalism.

Like the old fundamentalists before them, the new fundamentalists are a diverse group of people. They would agree with much of the old fundamentalist theology although many would be less willing to accept issues like the Bible's inspiration or the reality of miracles. They resist the stifling rigidity of the old fundamentalist mores and they recognize the freedom which we have in Christ (Gal. 5:1) but they seem to have forgotten that while all things are lawful, not all things are expedient or desirable for the follower of Christ (1 Cor. 6:12).

Like believers of fifty years ago, the new fundamentalists have a tendency to fall into the same behavior patterns which brought the old fundamentalism into such disrepute. For example the new fundamentalists often display:

Intellectual rigidity. Often there is no hesitation about reading sexually explicit novels or contemporary theology, but some modern Christian writers are ignored or dismissed *en toto* without their even being read or heard. This is not meant to defend contemporary Christian writers—often their weaknesses are very apparent—but intellectual honesty requires that before we criticize, condemn or reject contemporary evangelical communicators, they at least deserve a hearing.

Self-righteous superiority. Believing that they are free to attend X-rated movies, drink socially, or engage in other formerly taboo practices, some of the new fundamentalists flaunt this behavior. They are proud of their new-found freedom and intolerant of the "fundy-type of mentality" which still talks of separation from worldliness. Like the old fundamentalists, the new fundamentalists are in danger of developing a smug, intolerant, and exclusivist mentality which says, "We alone are right. Others are caught up in their old traditions and they lack the freedom which we are sophisticated enough to possess." Such an attitude leads to a new exclusivism and eccentric individualism in place of the old.

Indifference to churchmanship. Unlike the old fundamentalists who were rigid in church attendance but little concerned about the dignity of solemn worship, the new fundamentalists too often conclude that because the local church is dead, it can be avoided frequently and attended irregularly. An old habit of regular church attendance has been replaced by a habit of noninvolvement and attendance only when we feel like worshiping.

Unbalanced theology. Fundamentalists of old probably placed an overemphasis on individual Christian growth with a de-emphasis on social issues or on honest sharing within the body of Christ. The message of sin, repentance, and redemption was preached sometimes almost to the exclusion of an emphasis on divine love, mercy, and healing. The new fundamentalists reverse this process. Sin, divine wrath and the cost of discipleship are rarely stressed and there is a tendency to overemphasize *koinonia,* Christian love, social reform, and easy-believism theology.

De-emphasis on personal piety. The old fundamentalists put great stress on personal devotions—a daily period of prayer and

Bible study which was scheduled rigidly and missed only at the peril of experiencing great feelings of guilt. The new fundamentalist gives lip service to the importance of daily devotions but recognizes that circumstances may prevent rigid legalistic adherence to such a practice. As a result of this freer attitude, however, there often follows an elimination of personal devotions altogether with a resulting decline in spiritual vitality and sensitivity.

One of the most insightful Christian thinkers of our decade is a literary critic named Harry Blamires. His writing style is not easy to follow, but his insights are often profound and somewhat reminiscent of his Oxford professor and friend, C. S. Lewis.

In an examination of the Christian's position in this modern world, Blamires has concluded that we are faced with two major problems: "mental disorientation represented by the decline of doctrinal and institutional authority, and the cancer represented by the inner proliferation of malignant secularism, humanism, and materialism that corrode the vitals of the Christian body."[9] A loss of authority—especially biblical authority—and the acceptance of secular values has left us floundering. Instead of leading the world by giving moral direction and modeling commitment, we have silently merged with our pagan culture and have become indistinguishable from it.

Guidelines for the Christian Life Style

It is not possible and neither would it be wise to develop a list of rules which all believers would follow in order to have a truly Christian life style. Each of us is unique and we live in subcultures which are changing so rapidly that rules would be outdated quickly even if they could be devised. A better alternative is to seek biblically based guidelines for living and to apply these in our individual lives.

I am not implying that the following suggestions are in any way complete and neither do they consider the literally hundreds of specific principles for living which we find in the Bible. The following conclusions are, instead, a beginning set of general guidelines which can help us avoid the conforming mentality of easy believism and the old fundamentalism without slipping into the narrowness of new fundamentalism.

The Christian life style is characterized by holiness. Most of us probably feel uncomfortable with the label "holy." This word most often reminds us of God who is sinless and absolutely perfect—not like us—or the word raises somewhat negative thoughts about people who are "holy Joes," "holy rollers," or infected with a "holier-than-thou" pride.

According to the Bible, however, believers are instructed to be holy people. Nowhere is this more clearly seen than in Romans 12:1, 2—

> I urge you therefore, brethren, by the mercies of God, to present your bodies a living and holy sacrifice, acceptable to God, which is your spiritual service of worship. And do not be conformed to this world, but be transformed by the renewing of your mind, that you may prove what the will of God is, that which is good and acceptable and perfect.

The word "holy," as used in this quotation, does not mean absolutely perfect. To be holy is to be "set apart for God" with our lives "put at his disposal."[10] Of course, without divine help no human being can really live in a way that is acceptable and pleasing to God, but then we humans are never expected to become holy on our own. Instead, we are instructed to present ourselves completely to God, knowing that his Holy Spirit will then "set us apart" for special service, and will mold us into people who show love, joy, peace, patience, and other Christlike characteristics (Gal. 5:22, 23).

The Bible does not imply that we simply sit around, waiting for these changes to take place. We begin by asking the Holy Spirit to help us control our thinking. When we believers, in dependence on the Spirit, renovate our mental processes, then we begin to see changes in our outward actions and we can know and better conform to the will of God.

It is at the thinking level that the devil is most active and most subtle. He tempts us to think thoughts which are sinful but seemingly harmless because they are hidden from the view of everyone else. We fail to realize that when we let our minds dwell on sin, we find it easier to fall into sinful actions whenever there are temptations and opportunities to do so.

As we live and work in this busy world, it is easy to get caught up in the values and attitudes of our society and to forget that we are pilgrims who are "just passing through." Our hopes, aspirations, priorities, mannerisms, speech, habits, vocational goals and ways of spending both time and money should all reflect the fact that we are a people whose lives are set apart for service to God.

In finding a valid Christian life style, therefore, we must begin with constant reminders that we are holy people, set apart for special service. Then we must ask God to help us develop the habit of thinking thoughts which are pleasing to the one who has called us to be holy.

The Christian life style involves Christlike living. Near the turn of the century a man named Charles H. Sheldon wrote a novel which became a best seller.[11] The story describes a group of Christians who decided to take the words of 1 Peter 2:21 seriously: "Christ also suffered for you, leaving you an example, for you to follow in His steps."

How do we follow in his steps? The people in the story decided that they should preface every decision by asking, "What would Jesus do?" If we try, in every situation, to do what Jesus would do, then we have a valid guideline for Christian living.

Sheldon's novel is only fiction and the question—what would Jesus do?—has been criticized as an unrealistic formula for action.

I disagree. It is true that Jesus lived in a culture much simpler than ours, and it is possible to jump to unrealistic conclusions about how he would act if he lived among us today. Nevertheless, Christ is to be our model. We are to be like the Master and it can be helpful to ask what Jesus would do if he, for example, received a credit card in the mail, was driving in a 55 mph zone, was invited to attend a PG movie, was filling out his income tax form, was given the opportunity to become rich, was tired on Sunday morning, or was faced with the decision about whether to take a job which would consume his time and pull him away from family and church—but would also give an opportunity to help others in some unusual way.

In deciding our values, priorities, and ways of spending time, it can be helpful to ask ourselves—and other believers—"in a situation like this, what would Jesus do?"

The Christian life style involves caring and giving. One of the Bible stories which has influenced me the most concerns Jesus sitting near the offering box and watching as the worshipers made their donations. The wealthy made their impressive contributions but then a poor widow appeared and put in a pittance.

Jesus was most impressed with the widow. Unlike the people who gave "out of their wealth," the woman put in "all she had to live on" (Luke 21:1–4, NIV). Perhaps the wealthy givers had some self-centered values. Maybe, in their own minds they found "good" reasons for giving what they did. They may not have realized that God wants a willingness to commit everything to him. Jesus did not criticize these partial givers, and he appears to have said nothing to the woman, but he commented on her quiet act of dedication and made it clear to the disciples that he approved of her open, giving spirit.

Sometimes I think I'm like the people who give a part of what they own, but keep most for themselves. It could be argued, perhaps, that the widow didn't know how to manage her money very well, but her attitude is of greater importance. She was willing to give God everything.

To the human mind one of the most astonishing characteristics of God is the fact that he gives—without bargaining or vacillation. He gave his Son to die for our sins and, in turn, he loves those who give cheerfully and freely (2 Cor. 9:7; Matt. 10:8). Sixteen of the thirty-eight parables which Jesus told dealt with possessions, wealth, money, and our attitude toward riches. Jesus talked about the subject of money and possessions more than he discussed any other single theme—and the message was always the same: do not be controlled by a selfish love of things.

In the Sermon on the Mount, the giving of possessions appears to be as important as the giving of loving concern for others. "Give to everyone who asks of you . . ." Jesus proclaimed. "And just as you want men to treat you, treat them in the same way. . . . Love your enemies, and do good, and lend expecting nothing in return. . . . Give, and it will be given to you" (Luke 6:30, 31, 35, 38).

Here, then, is another principle for Christian living: Let your life be dominated by the golden rule and by a willingness to let all that you have be yielded to Christ.

This does not mean that I drop my entire paycheck into the offering plate; but it does mean that I have an attitude which really believes that everything I have belongs to God. This includes my money and possessions, but it also includes my talents, career, family, reputation, health, and even my life. Such commitment is not guaranteed to make life miserable and poverty-stricken—God has given us things to enjoy (1 Tim. 6:17). But such commitment does make life more complete and peaceful, because we are not in the struggle of deciding what God can have and what we will keep for ourselves. We acknowledge that all belongs to him.

The Christian life style involves pleasing God. Readers of the New Testament are often impressed with the depth and compassion shown in Paul's written prayers. In writing to the church at Colossae, for example, he told his readers that he prayed for them daily, asking that they would be

—filled with the knowledge of God's will,

—walking in a manner which pleases God

—involved in doing good work, and

—increasing in the knowledge of God (Col. 1:9, 10).

After giving a talk on the Christian life style, I was approached once by a man who suggested that Colossians 1:10 gives us the best guideline for daily living. In everything we do, we should ask God to lead us in such a way that our lives will always please God and honor him.

Conclusions about the Christian Life Style

Some people might argue that Christians who are young in years or faith can best be helped to follow Christ if they are given rules by which to live their lives. Rules can be stifling, however, and as people mature spiritually these rules become less helpful. It is better if they are replaced by general guidelines which can be used to mold attitudes, values, and life styles.

In living a Christian life, the major questions are not should I drink wine, use a credit card, watch movies with bad language, tithe or push to succeed in the business world. Instead all decisions about living are pushed through a sieve which retains only that which answers "yes" to some basic guideline questions:

- Do my actions and thoughts reflect the fact that I am a child of God, consecrated to him for special service?
- In making this decision about my actions and thoughts can I determine (by asking God, thinking about it, and sometimes seeking the help of other Christians) what Jesus would do?
- Do my actions and thoughts conform to the golden rule (Luke 6:31) and indicate a willingness to give and to care for others?

• Based on what I know about God, will my actions and thoughts be pleasing to him?

Mahatma Gandhi, the man whom we mentioned earlier, was not a Christian, but his life seemed to reflect these guidelines. How much more should we who name the name of Christ follow in the steps of the Savior?

When we reach the end of our pilgrimage, most of us will look back on a life which involved repeated failures and the frequent experience of God's forgiveness. How satisfying it will be if we can also recognize that we developed and lived a life style which shunned easy believism and truly was pleasing to Jesus Christ.

Those who are recognized as rulers . . .
lord it over them; and their great men
exercise authority over them. But it is
not so among you, but whoever wishes
to become great among you shall be
your servant; and whoever wishes to be
first among you shall be slave of all.

Mark 10:42–44

6
Selfless Success

Near the beginning of my years in graduate school, I began to
suspect that I was developing what might be called a "disease."
While it is common among people in all walks of life, it seems most
strongly to attack those who have spent some time in college. The
disease doesn't eat away at body tissues but it certainly puts a strain
on the pocketbook and sometimes on the eye muscles. At times I try
to fight the disease—which, for want of a better name, could be
called "compulsive book buying"—but like a thirsty kid at a pop
stand, I seem to succumb whenever I get near a bookstore. How
often, I wonder, have I gone into a bookstore "just to browse" and
come out with one or more books which I have convinced myself
that I need?

If I had time to read all of the books, these purchases might be
justified. Too often, however, the books sit on tables and desks
waiting to be read. One by one they find their way into the book-
shelves and sometimes, alas, they are forgotten—waiting for that
hoped-for "someday" when I will catch up with my reading.

Sometimes my book-buying all centers around a specific topic. A
couple of years ago, for example, when I was in the midst of a
colossal mid-life struggle, I purchased several books on success. I

had decided—this is typical of mid life—that I was a failure and it seemed wise to read something which could help me achieve some kind of success in the years which I might have left before retirement.

Unlike some of my other books, these guides to success didn't sit on the shelf unread. I started reading with enthusiasm and discovered, among other conclusions, that "all the virtues and all the joys of living are contained in one word—success."[1] I was informed that it is erroneous to assume that success spoils people since, on the contrary, it really makes us humble, tolerant, and kind.[2] I read a best-selling book by success expert Michael Korda who tells his readers how to dress, sit, stand, speak, act, relate to people, and think if they want to be successful. I also read Korda's philosophy for successful living. "You should not feel guilty. . . . You have a right to succeed. . . . Tell yourself: it's O.K. to be greedy. It's O.K. to be ambitious. It's O.K. to look out for Number One. . . . It's O.K. to recognize that honesty is not always the best policy. . . . It's O.K. to be a winner. And it's *always* O.K. to be rich."[3]

While few of the success writers were this blunt, most gave a variation of one standard message:

We *can* be successful.

We *can* get what we want.

The way to be successful is to change one's self-image, think positively, and learn how to manipulate other people.

It is true, no doubt, that most of us want to be successful and in itself there probably is nothing wrong with this desire. But we have become what one writer has described as a nation of individuals relentlessly pursuing success. It is our "respectable neuroses"—an intoxication characterized by the insatiable need to achieve.[4] When such thinking begins to permeate the Christian's thinking we become like the world around us—so consumed by a desire to "get ahead" that almost everything else fades in importance.

Although we each have our unique definitions of success, most of us would agree that in any one society there are features which clearly indicate who has "arrived."

The successful person in America, for example, has *visibility*. He or she has a high income and can spend money so conspicuously that everyone else can see the material evidences of success. In addition, the successful person has obvious *power* and *influence*, and for many it is also important to be *independent,* able to set our own hours and to come and go as we please.

The successful person in our society also has *self-control.* Outwardly, this is seen in people who know "how to handle" themselves, without showing incompetence or getting tongue-tied. Inwardly—according to those books on my shelves—the successful person is in control of his or her thinking. There is a positive mental attitude, an inner sense of confidence in what one is doing and a belief that one's work is self-fulfilling and "meaningful."

It may be stated less often but we generally assume that the successful person also has the *ability to control others.* When Ronald Reagan assumed the office of President of the United States, seasoned observers who may have disliked his policies nevertheless gave him credit for his charm and ability to persuade others to seriously consider and support his programs. Successful people often are able to manipulate others—sometimes so gently that few even recognize what is happening.

The Problem of Success

Since we live in a society which is saturated with this drive for achievement, I believe it is impossible for Christians to avoid the success mentality. We push our children to succeed in Little League, in school and in church contests. Even seminary students, committed to the ministry, find themselves struggling for grades, and moving into a competitive ecclesiastical world where (without ever saying this in words) they often struggle to have churches and ministries which are bigger than those of their former classmates.

According to church historian and seminary professor Richard Lovelace, the ultimate concern of most church members is not worship, service for Christ, evangelism, and social compassion. Instead, survival and success in one's secular vocation is of primary importance.

> Church members who have been conditioned all their lives to devote themselves to building their own kingdoms and whose flesh naturally gravitates in that direction anyway find it hard to invest much energy in the kingdom of God. They go to church once or twice a week and punch the clock, so to speak, fulfilling their "church obligation" by sitting passively and listening critically or approvingly to the pastor's teaching. . . .

> One cannot help but wonder what the result would be if this mass of lay people could be spiritually released from their servitude in the American success system and reoriented to channel their major energies toward building the kingdom of God.[5]

The success mentality which permeates and weakens our churches also affects us as individuals.

Like almost everyone else in the culture, believers have tended to tie their feelings of self-worth into their levels of achievement. We have accepted the subtle but destructive message that the only people who are worth anything are the people who succeed.

This conclusion is in stark contrast to biblical teaching which asserts clearly that we are valuable in God's sight whether we "succeed" or not.

This view that a person's intrinsic worth depends on his or her personal achievements can put us under tremendous pressure to "get ahead." A recent newspaper article described the growing problem of suicide among children in achievement-centered families. When they get poor grades, some of these students conclude that they aren't worth anything, so they kill themselves. They have never learned that God's love and acceptance is unconditional—not dependent on what we have accomplished.

The drive for success is made more stressful because we all realize that there isn't much room at the top. Most people will not achieve it in terms of the world's standards. We may all convince ourselves that we are "better than average"[6] and that "while others won't make it, I will." Nevertheless we know that worldly success is for the very few and that riches and being born in the "right" family may have more influence on success than does hard work and good grades.[7]

Even those who do reach the top discover that there is often a price to be paid for success. Fame and status can lead to pride and restricted privacy. Money can control us and lead to greed and a love for possessions which can cause "all sorts of evil" (1 Tim. 6:10). Accomplishments and acclaim from others can put us under tremendous pressure to "keep up" to past levels of achievement. This was expressed succinctly by a famous novelist who won a Nobel prize for his work, but who admitted in a television interview: "I have now reached the height of success, but from here on everybody will expect me to write Nobel-prize quality literature. I'm not sure I can do this! I don't want such pressure!"

For Christians, however, the modern success-mentality presents an even greater problem. Success, as defined by the world around us and as pursued by millions, is in vivid contrast to and in clear conflict with biblical teaching.

The Bible and Success

The word "success" is rarely mentioned in the Scriptures. Abraham's servant prayed for success when he went to find a bride for Isaac (Gen. 12:24). Joseph was described as a "successful" man (Gen. 39:2) and God gave Joshua some principles for success following the death of Moses (Josh. 1:7, 8). Later in biblical history, Nehemiah expressed confidence that God would give him success in rebuilding the walls of Jerusalem (Neh. 2:20) and Daniel is described as a man who "enjoyed success" (Dan. 6:28), but nothing is said about the meaning of success or about how it could be handled. The word "success" never even appears in the New Testament, but from this it does not follow that success was of no concern to the early believers.

Although the *word* "success" is rare in Scripture, the *idea* of success is mentioned frequently. When two men asked Jesus for a place of prominence in his kingdom, he rebuked them and announced that such status-seeking is a non-Christian value. What is a common view in the world "is not so among you," he proclaimed. "Whoever wishes to become great among you shall be your servant" (Matt. 20:26).

Elsewhere, Jesus taught that it is futile to gain the whole world and lose everything spiritually (Matt. 16:26). He emphasized that loving God and helping our neighbor were the most important ingredients to life (Matt. 22:37–40); that status-seeking leads to pride which must give way to a humble attitude and a willingness to serve others (Matt. 23:1–12); that we must be faithful in using the gifts which come from God (Matt. 25:21) and that our major purpose in life is to make disciples (Matt. 28:19, 20). Each of us has a responsibility not to knock down others in a stampede to the top, but to be a faithful investor of the talents and opportunities which God has given. The words of Jesus are clear on these issues:

> No servant can serve two masters; for either he will hate the one, and love the other, or else he will hold to one, and despise the other. You cannot serve God and Mammon (or riches).

Now the Pharisees, who were lovers of money, were listening to all these things, and they were scoffing at Him.

And He said to them, "You are those who justify yourselves in the sight of men, but God knows your hearts; for that which is highly esteemed among men is detestable in the sight of God.

(Luke 16:13–16)

The Sermon on the Mount carries a similar message, warning against the pursuit of possessions and the anxiety over security (Matt. 6:19–21; 31–33). The writer of Hebrews lists worship and "doing good and sharing" as the really important purposes for life (Heb. 13:15, 16), while the writer of James condemns "selfish ambition," jealousy, and pride (James 3:13–18; 4:10, 14).

I once did a brief study of the "successful" people in Scripture—people like Joshua, Elijah, Job, Mary, and John the Baptist. Only a few—like Joseph and Daniel—fit our modern descriptions of the successful individual and clearly that success was given by God, not to honor the "successful" saint, but to bring honor to the Lord and to accomplish his purposes. My study led me to conclude that according to Scripture the successful Christian:

- consistently acknowledges God's sovereignty and power;
- seeks to please God (that is our prime ambition—2 Cor. 5:9);
- serves, does good, cares for, builds up and encourages others (Gal. 5:13; 6:9, 10; 1 Cor. 12:25; 1 Thess. 5:11);
- does not strive for status, acclaim, riches or possessions;
- trusts God to provide needs;
- humbly recognizes, accepts, develops, and uses God-given gifts, strengths, and abilities;
- does not resist being used by God, even if this means the accumulation of worldly goods and status;
- avoids jealousy or coveting a position of prominence and realizes that God gives responsibilities, gifts and status as he wills (Ps. 75:5–7; 1 Cor. 12:4–18; Gal. 5:24–26); and
- is aware of the fact that dedicated service to God does not always bring worldly success—sometimes persecution and hardship result instead (Heb. 11:32–40).

As you read this list, perhaps your reaction was like mine as I wrote it: that no one can possibly attain such a state of selfless dedication. Perhaps this is true, but with God's help we can get closer and closer to the goal as we grow in spiritual maturity.

One of my daughters is an ice skater. She practices regularly and works at her various assignments, but she will never be perfect. Even Olympic gold medalists feel that they could improve, and the more they train, the better they get. Attitudes and actions which were very difficult to remember and to practice in the early days, slowly become ingrained and automatic as the skaters improve. Everyone can see the improvement, even though the athlete is far short of the ideal.

The guidelines which direct our Christian lives are not intended to fill us with guilt and to immobilize us with feelings of failure. Christian standards, instead, are meant to give us direction and goals which can challenge us and make life more meaningful.

The Essence of Greatness and Success

About three years ago, I was invited to speak to the honors society of a nearby Christian college on the topic of "greatness." I prepared carefully for the talk but the evening remains in my memory as one of my most blatant failures as a speaker. The reason for this may have rested partially with the audience—they were highly intelligent people who clearly were impressed with their capabilities and apparently took great pride in the fact that they had been elected to the honor society. Even before my speech was over, however, I recognized that much of the reason for my failure could also have rested on me. During the dinner and "induction of new members" ceremony which preceded the speaker, I concluded that this was a stuffy group and I wasn't surprised when they turned out to be a most unresponsive audience.

After that meeting I began to ponder what it really means to be great. I don't know if I've met any really great people, but I have had contact with a few individuals who seem to come close to that ideal.

Paul Tournier, the renowned Swiss counselor and writer, is an example. When I first met the man he didn't impress me with his intellect, his ego, or his style of dress. I was impressed instead with his sensitivity and sincere concern for people. Most of all, I was overwhelmed with his deep humility—a humility which seemed all the more real when I discovered later that the man considers a battle with pride to be one of his biggest personal struggles.

Tournier would not consider himself to be "great"; few, if any, really great people would apply such a label to themselves. It is possible, however, that he would agree that truly great people show at least ten characteristics.

Once again, these are listed as one set of guidelines. They give us a goal toward which we can aim and are not presented as impossible standards which are designed to make us all feel like failures. People who are great or who show potential for greatness are not always rich, famous, or members of the college honor society. Instead they seem to be growing in the following areas:

1. *Excellence.* Psychologist John Gardner, a Republican member of Lyndon Johnson's Democratic cabinet, wrote a little book in the 1960s which became required reading in many college classrooms.

Gardner maintained that a society cannot achieve greatness unless individuals at all levels of ability set high standards of performance and strive, as best they can, to achieve these standards. The successful person is he or she who constantly strives for excellence—if not in all areas, then at least in some—and who recognizes both that perfection will not be possible, and that nothing permanent is to be gained by "beating out" someone else in a compulsive drive to get ahead.

Gardner perceptively recognized that

. . . extreme emphasis on performance as a criterion of status may foster an atmosphere of raw striving that results in brutal treatment of the less able, or less vigorous, or less aggressive; it may wantonly injure those whose temperament or whose values make them unwilling to engage in performance rivalries; it may penalize those whose undeniable excellences do not add up to the kinds of performance that society at any given moment chooses to reward.[8]

Several years ago, our family visited Prague and we determined to purchase some Czechoslovakian glass as a souvenir. The saleslady spoke quietly but was remarkably candid in her comments about our purchase.

"You can't get glass here like it used to be. The workers no longer strive for quality. Turning out second-rate materials is one of the few ways in which they can resist the communist dictatorship."

In the West, I suspect, we have other reasons for a decline in excellence and a reduced pride in our work. To state it bluntly, many people are too lazy, too self-centered, too caught up in "the narcotic of easy living and the distractions of a well-heeled society."[9] We have concluded that happiness involves ease and tranquillity and we have forgotten that true satisfaction comes as we work toward meaningful goals.

In addition, we have elevated some professions and callings to a place of high status and seem to have concluded that excellence is only possible in some areas of endeavor. John Gardner challenges this creatively:

> An excellent plumber is infinitely more admirable than an incompetent philosopher. The society which scorns excellence in plumbing because plumbing is a humble activity and tolerates shoddiness in philosophy because it is an exalted activity will have neither good plumbing nor good philosophy. Neither its pipes nor its theories will hold water.[10]

To be excellent does not mean that we are to be superior to others or that we succeed in everything we do. I don't think God evaluates us on the basis of whether or not we have made it to the top of our professions, become famous or earned a lot of money. God is concerned with who we are and what we are becoming. If we have a desire for growth and a vision for excellence, he enables us to become the people *he* wants us to be.

2. *Dissatisfaction.* Think of the people—alive or in our historical past—whom you consider to be truly great. It is likely that all of these heroes had a rebellious streak within. They may not have been tearing down society or engaging in character assassination, but these people probably have been dissatisfied with the status quo. They have observed the needs and injustice around them and, like Jesus, they have determined to bring about changes.

Such people are not always popular. Jesus wasn't!

They are bold enough to ask questions, however, honest enough to hear new ideas, and usually courageous enough to do something rather than sitting back passively and letting things drift along from bad to worse.

3. *Vision.* In the 1960s when I began my teaching career, campuses all over the world were in turmoil. Militant students were throwing rocks, taking over the deans' offices, and bodily removing administrators.

These students were dissatisfied but they had no vision. They were intent on tearing down society—they called it the "military-industrial complex"—but they had no plans or creative ideas for making it better. They had become a modern example of King

Solomon's ancient wisdom: "Where there is no vision, the people are unrestrained" (Prov. 29:18).

Sometimes, it seems, we become rigid, lethargic, and cynical in our view of the world. I have seen this in some of my older friends. They know that things are unlikely to change, so they withdraw into a world devoid of creative ideas. Their employers often like this—it can be threatening to preside over a corporation, university, or even a church or mission, if some of the people within keep raising visionary ideas. In contrast, surely, it is significant that the prophet Joel and the apostle Peter talked positively about young men who see visions (Joel 2:28–32; Acts 2:17). Without creative visions, individuals and societies dry up in musty deterioration.

4. *Action.* It is possible to believe in excellence, to be dissatisfied with the status quo, to have creative visionary ideas, and then to do nothing. Such inactivity is not the mark of success or of greatness.

Potentially great people step out and do what they can to bring change. In doing so these people take a risk. They might get criticized or ostracized. They might fail and say or do things which they will regret later. Like the old cliché proclaims, however, these people have decided that it is better to try and to fail than never to try at all.

I once worked with a man who was impressed with the evangelist Billy Graham. "I want to be like Dr. Graham," my friend admitted one day. "I want to have the right image as a Christian leader. I want to dress properly, to have my letters typed accurately, and to speak powerfully."

I admired my friend's desire for excellence but I didn't admire his apparent motive: to have the impeccable image of doing everything "just right."

One day I asked a member of Dr. Graham's staff if the evangelist was really concerned about image. The answer was revealing.

"He is most concerned about deciding what is right—*and doing it!*" That is a mark of greatness. It is deciding what needs to be done and taking action even though such action could lead to failure.

5. *Communication Ability.* Almost every book or article concerning marriage problems, family tension, and interpersonal relations deals, at some point, with the importance of communication.

Almost all of these writers also note that communication is not easy. It involves sensitivity to others, careful listening, trying to lay aside our personal biases, expressing our ideas concisely, and using language which others can understand. The good communicator does not jump to conclusions and neither does he or she give "double messages"—saying one thing with the lips and giving a different message with one's actions and behavior.

I'm not sure where we got the strange idea that people who are brilliant and scholarly should use vague and difficult words. Jesus spoke in the language of the people. He used parables and examples to help them understand. At times he may have used technical terms which some people missed, but in general his communication was simple, without being simplistic.

6. *Self-discipline*. I once knew a student who described a very common problem.

"I'm 27 years old and I haven't learned a thing about discipline. I get up late. I eat a lot of junk food and don't bother to get exercise. My spiritual life is an off-again, on-again (mostly off-again) type of relationship. I only pray when I feel like it. I don't plan ahead. I cram for exams and stay up all night when an assignment is due— then I coast. In a word, I don't have any discipline."

Sometimes I get the impression that in the previous century, discipline was indistinguishable from rigidity and unchangeable rules of behavior. Twentieth-century men and women resisted binds like that and went from too much discipline to a state of almost no discipline at all. Our schools advocated a nonstructured type of learning and people even began to talk about "free love"—which was not restrained by the ties of marriage. Even Christians began to emphasize freedom in Christ and that sometimes translated into "freedom from discipline."

But freedom and discipline are not opposites. In a recent book, Richard Foster titles his first chapter, "Spiritual Disciplines: Door to Liberation" and notes that all of the great spiritual leaders affirmed the necessity of disciplines—such as prayer, service and meditation—if we are to mature freely.[11] An undisciplined life is really wasteful and unproductive[12]—both personally and spiritually. Without discipline, we become slaves to our whims and impulses. We really are not free.

My student friend recognized that without discipline, little of value is accomplished in this life. He made his own lack of discipline a matter for prayer. He began getting up at regular times, made a list of his goals, and started scheduling his work day. He found a couple of friends who could encourage and prod him—and he went on to get his doctor's degree primarily because he had learned to discipline his time and energies.

7. *Persistence.* When I went through graduate school I decided that it takes more than self-discipline to get a degree. It takes the ability to stick with a task until it is done.

Persistence is difficult; giving up is easy. Whether you are learning to play the piano, going through a training program, writing a book, (or even reading one) or building a house—there is a tendency to get halfway through and want to quit. Great people, and successful ones, resist that temptation. Without being rigid they nevertheless keep plugging along until they reach their goals.

8. *Balance.* A magazine editor once asked me to write an article to be titled "Balancing a Man's Life." That was a difficult assignment both to write about and to apply in day-to-day living.

To keep a balance in life we need to be diligent in our work (without becoming workaholics), sensitive to our families, willing to take time off—even if this means doing nothing at times—devoted to prayer and meditation, and involved with Christian service.

It is easy for life to get unbalanced. Without giving it much thought our work, church activities, leisure pursuits, sometimes our families and perhaps even our personal devotions can take so much time that we become like a monster with one part of the body grown out of proportion to the rest. Most of us need God's help to live a balanced life.

9. *Godliness.* Almost a decade ago, our family went to live in Switzerland while I did research for a book. We settled in Geneva and discovered almost immediately that four centuries after his death, the influence of John Calvin is still felt in that great city.

At the time of our visit, I knew almost nothing about Calvin, so I purchased a short biography and on Sunday afternoons we began to visit the places in Geneva where Calvin had lived and taught and ministered.

One day I was walking through our little apartment and glanced at the biography of Calvin which was sitting on an end table. I had already read the book but its title had not grabbed my attention until that momentary glance. Writing 400 years after the great reformer's death, the author had chosen to title the book *The Man God Mastered.*[13]

I stopped abruptly and began to ponder the title. Calvin had died centuries before, but in spite of the criticisms which still surround his work he was being remembered as a man God mastered. Would anyone ever think that about me? More important, would God ever think that during my lifetime Gary Collins became a man God mastered?

At about that time I was reading the Epistles of Peter and discovered that God, by his divine power, has already given us what we need to be godly sharers of the divine nature (2 Peter 1:4, 5). We do not sit idly by and wait for God to transform us, however. With all diligence and energy, the Christian, beginning with faith in Jesus Christ, must develop moral excellence (the courage to show whose we are and whom we serve);[14] knowledge which enables us to "decide rightly and efficiently in the day-to-day circumstances and situations of life";[15] self-control and self-mastery; a brave and courageous perseverance; piety—which involves devout worship of God and a duty to serve God and our fellow-men;[16] brotherly kindness; and a Christlike love (2 Peter 1:6, 7).

Some writers have called this a "ladder of virtues." If life is geared toward climbing this ladder and developing these traits we will be useful and fruitful in this life. We will be people who are great and successful in God's eyes. We will be godly—men and women whom God masters (2 Peter 1:8).

The alternative is to be short-sighted Christians who walk through life blinking and stumbling spiritually. We may reach the top of the world's ladder of success and may gain fame and riches. Ultimately, however, this glory fades. Ultimate, lasting success and greatness only come when we concentrate on the more difficult but infinitely more important "ladder of virtues" which God helps us climb if we really want to reach the top.

10. *Humility.* Would it be correct to conclude that all really great people are also humble? Certainly humility characterized Jesus, the greatest person who ever lived, and in lesser forms it radiates from the lives of the more recent great.

As we have seen, the brother of Jesus criticized arrogance and selfish ambition (James 3:14), urging instead that Christ's followers should humble themselves. The result is that Christ, in turn, will lift us up (James 4:10). How could any of us be more certain of success and greatness than to be "exalted" by Christ himself? The path to true greatness is through humility; the mark of true greatness is humility.

To this ten-point blueprint, we could have added intelligence, education, knowledge of one's field, sensitivity to people, and a host of other characteristics which are important but surely of secondary significance. It is also worth noting that great people often don't recognize their own influence and few if any of the truly great have a concern about "getting known" or "making a name" for themselves. If they are Christians, they are more concerned about finding God's will and doing it. That is success!

Working toward Success

One of my friends is a dedicated Christian, an astute businessman and a gentle critic of how we "run" our churches. Through his work as an outside accountant for many churches my friend has discovered that, without meaning to do so, many churches break the law repeatedly in the way they handle money. Many pastors who are dedicated and well meaning use terrible business practices and violate every rule of sound management as they lead the local body of believers.

I would hate to think that as an alternative to such inefficiency churches should completely adopt professional management principles, and be organized like corporations. Churches, as believers who comprise the body of Christ, exist to bring glory to God. Unlike business corporations, the church accepts the walking wounded, the skilled and the unskilled, the educated and the untaught, the mature and the childish. We cannot run the church, or our lives, as a strict business venture, but we can develop some goals and priorities which enable our lives and worship to be more fruitful and "successful"—in the best meaning of that word.

Ted W. Engstrom has suggested that two priorities must take precedence before we start thinking about our "work for God."[17] First, we must make time for communion with God, and then we must determine to share freely with our families and with our fellow believers. Having accepted these priorities, it then becomes helpful to establish more specific purposes and goals.

Purposes, according to Engstrom, are general statements about the future. They are ideals toward which we strive and may involve such aspirations as these: I want to be great, mastered by God, more patient with my family, a better businessman or writer, a good mother, more involved in church, a better athlete or student. Each of these is a statement of what we want to be; each gives a direction for our lives, but each is somewhat vague. How will we know, for example, when we are mastered by God or "more involved" in the church? To make these purposes more specific we must break them down into goals.

Goals are more specific, achievable, and easier to manage. They are statements about what we believe God wants us to do or to be "in light of his word."

In planning for the future, it can be helpful to follow a four-part guideline.

1. *Take some time to list priorities.* In doing this, I found it helpful to take several sheets of paper which I labeled "Spiritual Life," "Family," "Finances," "Vocation," and "Writing." Then, on each sheet I listed some priorities. Under "Family," for example, I wrote:

To honor God through our family

To model, demonstrate and teach Christian values and standards in the home

To be a good husband, father and son

To have fun in our family

Periodically I pull out my lists and update them.

2. *Based on these priorities, write down some goals.* Well written goals are

—specific and definite as to what is expected

—achievable in a certain time span

—practical and feasible

—stated in terms of quantity when possible

—limited to one goal in each statement.

On my family page, "to take each of my daughters out to breakfast once a month for the next year" would be a specific goal.

It may take some time to write clear goals and according to Engstrom we get bogged down when our goal statements are vague in terms of what is expected (e.g. "to spend time with my children"); idealistic ("to be super as a father"); too complicated; too long; and without any dates which tell when we will start and finish.

Some of the goals might be long range ("to get a college degree within the next five years") while others may be more immediate—to be accomplished today, this month, or within the next year.

When your list is made ask these questions about each goal:[18]

- Is this goal *accomplishable:* do you believe you can do it (under God's leading)?
- Does this goal have a date: will you know when you want to do it?
- Is this goal *measurable:* will you know that it has in fact been achieved?
- Does this goal have *steps* (a plan): do you know how to reach it?
- Is this goal *claimed:* do you know who will be responsible for following the plan?
- Is this goal *supported:* do we have the financial resources to accomplish it?

3. *Now put your goals in order of priority.* Beside each goal put an A for "must do" goals, a B for "should do," and a C for "would be nice to do" goals.

Then look at your A-level goals and decide what you can do now to start moving forward. Be specific in your planning and remember that because we are limited in time, energy, money, and abilities, we can't do everything.

4. *Start working on the goals.* A list of goals which doesn't spur you to action is a useless list. Making lists of "to do" projects can lull you into thinking that progress is being made, but until you start checking off "achieved goals" on your list, you are still at the planning stage.

In all of this planning, there is a need to be both persistent and flexible. Our perceptions change periodically, new opportunities present themselves, and we see the world differently as we grow older. God's leading may also direct us to shift goals and priorities. Therefore, in an attitude of prayerful deliberation, it is wise to return to our lists frequently and make some revisions.

It also is wise to remember these words from a brilliant Old Testament writer:

Commit your works to the Lord
And your plans will be established. . . .
The mind of man plans his way,
But the Lord directs his steps (Prov. 16:3, 9).

In all of our planning we must ask and expect that God will lead in the direction which he wants our lives to take. We can never be sure of our future circumstances on earth. "You do not know what your life will be like tommorow. You are just a vapor that appears for a little while and then vanishes away. Instead, you ought to say, 'If the Lord wills, we shall do this or that' " (James 4:14, 15). With this perspective in mind we can plan ahead while we also acknowledge God's will and sovereignty.

Dealing with Success

In a world which puts such high value on success, it can be helpful to ask ourselves some basic questions about where we fit. *How does all of this apply now?* Regardless of one's age or station in life it can be helpful to keep planning carefully for the future—perhaps in terms of the guidelines proposed in this chapter: aim high, striving for excellence; prepare fully for the future—and keep learning; expect that God will guide; and continually thank him for the opportunities for service that he gives.

What if I don't succeed, according to the world's standards? Never forget that God loves and accepts us, regardless of what the world thinks. Our prime goal must be to please him. Someday we will see him in person and live—mortgage free—in the dwelling places which Christ has prepared for us (John 14:1–3).

What if I am successful according to the world's standards? If this happens, keep a humble attitude by recognizing that it is God who has given you the abilities, the opportunities, and even the "drive" to get ahead. Those ancient words of Jeremiah are worth repeating.

> "Let not a wise man boast of his wisdom; and let not the mighty man boast of his might, let not the rich man boast of his riches; but let him who boasts boast of this; that he understands and knows Me, that I am the Lord who exercises lovingkindness, justice, and righteousness on earth; for I delight in these things," declares the Lord (Jer. 9:23, 24).

A few years ago I was invited to speak to a group of booksellers on the subject of success. I worked hard in preparing for the task, but the night before the meeting, my own distorted views of success convicted me with great force as I looked over my notes in the motel room. My prayer, that night, was one that I never want to forget:

"Lord, thank you for the abilities, creativity, vision, enthusiasm, and opportunities which you alone have given and which contribute toward the degree of success which I have. Please help me always to be

- grateful to God (without pride)
- gracious to others (without insensitivity, superficiality, or a lack of concern), and
- genuine with myself (without that stress-producing drive to reach the top of the world's success ladder)."

Grateful, gracious, and genuine—these are three traits that I want to characterize my life. I pray for them almost every day. *What if my life still seems disjointed?* One of my favorite authors is Henri Nouwen, a Dutch-born Roman Catholic priest who has taught and written widely in the area of pastoral psychology and theology.

At one point in his life, Nouwen began to recognize that his life was caught in a "web of strange paradoxes." His vocation of being a witness to God's love was turning into a tiring job. He was lecturing and writing about the importance of solitude, inner freedom, and peace of mind, but he knew that his life was characterized by compulsions, tension, and restless searching. He found that he was speaking more about God than with him. Writing about prayer had kept Nouwen from a prayerful life. With refreshing honesty he wrote that he was becoming more concerned about the praise of men and women than about the love of God. He realized that he

. . . was slowly becoming a prisoner of people's expectations instead of a man liberated by divine promises. . . . I had succeeded in surrounding myself with so many classes to prepare, lectures to give, articles to finish, people to meet, phone calls to make, and letters to answer, that I had come quite close to believing that I was indispensable.

When I took a closer look at this I realized that . . . while complaining about too many demands, I felt uneasy when none were made. While speaking about the burden of letter writing, an empty mailbox made me sad. . . . While speaking nostalgically about an empty desk, I feared the day on which that would come true. In short: while desiring to be alone, I was frightened of being left alone. The more I became aware of these paradoxes, the more I started to see how much I had indeed fallen in love with my own compulsions and illusions, and how much I needed to step back and wonder, "Is there a quiet stream underneath the fluctuating affirmations and rejections of my little world? Is there a still point where my life is anchored and from which I can reach out with hope and courage and confidence?"[19]

To find answers, Nouwen decided to live for seven months as a guest in a Trappist monastery in upstate New York. At the end of each day he recorded his observations in a diary which shows unusual candor, perhaps because it was not prepared originally as a manuscript to be published.

After several weeks in the monastery, Nouwen began to get a clearer perspective on his career and his attitudes toward success. "How divided my heart has been," he wrote in a notation which many of us could also claim.

I want to love God, but also to make a career. I want to be a good Christian, but also to have my successes as a teacher, preacher, or speaker. I want to be a saint but also enjoy the sensations of a sinner. I want to be close to Christ but also popular and liked by many people. No wonder that living becomes a tiring enterprise. . . . I . . . am double-hearted, double-minded, and have a very divided loyalty.

"Set your hearts on his kingdom first . . . and all these other things will be given you as well" (Mt. 6:33). Jesus is very clear about it. You cannot love God and mammon, you cannot be for him and against him, you cannot follow him just a little bit. Everything or nothing. . . .

If I could slowly come to that trust in God, that surrender, that childlike openness, many tensions, and worries would fall away, would be unmasked as false, empty, unnecessary worries, not worth the time and energy, and I could live a simple life. . . . Then I would have an open mind, open to perceive many things I didn't notice before, open to hear many people I didn't hear before. Then I wouldn't worry about my name, my career, my success, my popularity and would be open to the voice of God and his people. Then I probably also would know much better what is worth doing and what is not, which lectures to accept and which to refuse, which people to spend time with and which people to keep at a distance. Then I most likely would be less plagued by passions causing me to read the wrong books, hang around the wrong places, and waste my time with the wrong company. Then—no doubt—I would have much more time to pray, to read, to study, and to be always prepared to speak the word of God when the right time has come. Wherever I am . . . I would not feel irritated, restless, and desirous of being somewhere else or doing something else. I would know that here and now is what counts and is important because it is God himself who wants me at this time in this place.[20]

Most of us don't have the time or opportunity to withdraw for several months to a place of contemplation. But even brief periods of meditation can help to keep our views of success in a balanced perspective. Like Saul on the road to Damascus, our constant prayer must be, "Lord, here I am. What do you want me to do?" Such a prayer, honestly offered, is always answered.

A new commandment I give to you,
that you love one another, even as I
have loved you, that you also love one
another. By this all men will know that
you are My disciples, if you have love
for one another.

John 13:34, 35

And this is love, that we walk according to His commandments . . .

2 John 6

7

Giving Love

You can learn a lot about people by listening to their speech. The ways in which educated people express themselves tend to differ from the grammar used by those who are less educated. People who swear a lot frequently have values which are different from those of nonswearers. Many vocations—like medicine or the military—have a jargon which may have little meaning to people who work some-place else, but is understood completely by insiders. Although most of us lack the linguistic expertise to tell—simply by listening—where some other person grew up, we still can recognize the distinc-tive sound of a Southern, New England, British, Irish, or non-English "foreign" accent.

Even the use of distorted language can be revealing. When I was in Thailand several years ago, riding in a Bangkok taxi, an Ameri-can friend wanted to make a comment which could have been mis-understood by our driver.

"Ary-gay," my friend began, "An-kay, ou-yay, eek-spay, ig-pay, atin-lay?"*

---

*Translation: "Gary, can you speak pig latin?"

I replied that I knew a little "pig latin." (We learned as children to communicate by putting the first consonant at the end of each word.) Thus we were able to carry on our brief conversation, because we shared some common experiences in our upbringing and knew of a way to communicate without using normal English language sounds.

I mention all of this because language has become one important way by which we determine whether or not other people are really similar to us or different. Nowhere perhaps do we see this more clearly than in the area of religion.

I once co-authored an article with a friend who is a Catholic priest. It was clear that Father Glynn and I shared many of the same beliefs but we expressed ourselves using different words. This made our writing task more difficult because we weren't always able to understand each other.

Nonbelievers and new Christians often find a special jargon when they come into our churches. Sometimes these people are confused and even feel ostracized because they have no idea what it means to "make a decision for Christ," "get saved," "be discipled," or (even worse) to understand "predestination," "sanctification," and a "pretribulation premillennial rapture." The more we meet together and use such words, the more we develop our own "in-group" language. It is possible to reach a point where we can't communicate with nonbelievers and it is easy to start questioning the orthodoxy of people who don't speak like we do. Often without thinking about this consciously, we conclude that the mark of a true believer is his or her ability to use "our" jargon. We fail to realize that some people may say the "right" words but not be believers, while others who use unfamiliar terms, nevertheless love and serve the same Lord whom we worship.

The Bible does not say that a true believer can be detected by the way in which he or she speaks. Instead, there is one way to know if someone is really a follower of Christ. The distinguishing mark of a true Christian is difficult to miss because it has been stated so clearly by Jesus (John 13:34–35), John (1 John 3:11; 4:7, 8, 12, 19–21), and Paul (Rom. 13:8; 1 Cor. 13:13; Gal. 5:13–15). *The chief characteristic of the Christian is love.* Consider for example these powerful words:

> A new commandment I give to you, that you love one another, even as I have loved you, that you also love one another.

By this shall all men know that you are My disciples, if you have love for one another (John 13:34, 35).
The one who does not love does not know God . . . if we love one another, God abides in us . . .
If someone says, "I love God," and hates his brother, he is a liar; for one who does not love his brother whom he has seen, cannot love God whom he has not seen (1 John 4:8, 12, 20).

The Art of Loving: Love Described

Erich Fromm was a famous and controversial psychoanalyst who wrote numerous books but probably is best known for a slim little volume titled *The Art of Loving.*[1] Fromm believed that we don't just "turn love on" or fall into love. Love, he wrote, is not just a sentiment which anyone can experience regardless of maturity level. Instead, if we really want to love, Fromm believed that we must work to develop the total personality. We cannot love, unless our lives are characterized by "humility, courage, faith and discipline."[2] These qualities are rare, Fromm concluded, but so is the true capacity to love.

Love may be the most confusing and misunderstood word in the English language. Most often it refers to some mixture of what we like, what we find attractive, and what arouses us sexually. Without hesitation a man can use the one word "love" to describe his feelings about chocolate milkshakes, camping trips in the wilderness, and sexual relations with his wife. We use the same word "to describe romance, affection, compassion, and enjoyment; as well as to describe our relationship to Almighty God."[3] Sometimes love becomes a vague synonym for the "happiness" or "fulfillment" which countless people pursue but never find.

Recognizing that no concise definition of love can ever be possible, George Sweeting nevertheless appears to be accurate in stating that love is "that divine force that draws a man to God and to men and women who are made in the image of God. And we can only know this wonderful love as we know God."[4]

More detailed is Fromm's division of love into five types: brotherly love, motherly love, erotic love, self-love, and love of God.[5] This contrasts with the work of Funderburk who based his conclusions on a biblical study instead of on psychological analysis, and writes about family love, friendship love, spurious (selfish) love, and spiritual love.[6]

Better known, perhaps, are the "four loves" described by C. S. Lewis.[7] *Affection,* the most basic and perhaps the most superficial type of love, involves a warm but sometimes fleeting preference for another person or thing. *Friendship* is a deeper relationship between persons who share common ideas, desires or values. *Eros,* which means "being in love," involves sexual attraction, arousal, and intercourse—although it is possible both to have sex without love and love without sex. The fourth love, *charity,* is a love which comes from God and is described most accurately in 1 Corinthians 13.

It is widely known that the Greek language had three words for love: eros, philia and agape. The first of these, *eros,* never appears in the Bible. It is a word which refers to physical pleasure. This tends to be short-lived and often self-centered. It is, writes C. S. Lewis, "the kind of love that lovers are in." Of course, erotic love can be very pleasurable. It is a powerful example of the marvelous complexity of human beings, but it is not the kind of love that occupies the attention of New Testament writers.

Philia is a compassionate love which involves liking and a sincere fondness for some other person. Sometimes called "brotherly love," this is an emotional feeling of affection which brings a lot of "solid genuine happiness" into our lives.[8]

Agape is seldom found in classical Greek—perhaps because the Greeks saw it so seldom—but it permeates the pages of Scripture. It has been called the word which is most characteristic of Christianity. "It is employed in expressing God's love for human beings (John 3:16); human love for God (2 Thess. 3:5; 1 John 2:5, 3:17); and our spiritual love for others (John 15:12; Rom. 13:8; Gal. 5:14)."[9] Agape love involves a concern for the welfare of others. It leads us to acts of benevolence and good will both in our thinking and behaving. It is not a natural characteristic of human beings but comes from God to believers who love, because Christ loved us first (1 John 4:19).

Philia and agape have overlapping meaning, but in one respect the words are different. Philia is an emotion, and since emotions cannot be turned on or off at will, we are never commanded to love this kind of love. Agape, in contrast, involves acts of kindness which we can show whether we feel like it or not. We are instructed to be characterized by such acts of loving.[10] And when we act in loving ways, the positive feelings often follow.

The Art of Serving: Love Expressed

Early in our Christian lives, most of us learn that "God is very loving (1 John 4:7, 8)." In the most familiar verse of the Bible (John 3:16) we are told that Jesus Christ was sent to the world because of God's love for us. Jesus himself was so loving that he gave his life for a sinful world (John 15:13) and after he went back into heaven, the early church learned that we should follow Christ's example and work "in love," like he did (Eph. 5:3; Col. 3:19).

But how do we work in love? How can people like us really show love when most of us are more inclined to be self-centered, sometimes critical, and often too busy to show much concern for other people? The answer to these questions is found both in the example of Jesus and in the commandments of Scripture.

Jesus demonstrated love by being a servant. "The Son of man did not come to be served, but to serve," he told his disciples (Mark 10:45). In a world filled with pious religious leaders, Jesus could have demanded special celebrity status. Instead, he criticized the hypocrites of his day, showed genuine care for the needy and once, with a towel and basin of water, he went around the room washing the feet of his disciples.

It has been suggested that in describing his humanity, Jesus only used two words:[11] "I am gentle and humble" (Matt. 11:29). His whole life reflected that self-description.

Jesus told us to love by being servants. In what has been called "one of the most revealing passages in the New Testament"[12] Jesus once gave a startling lesson about the Christian life style (Matt. 20:20–28).

The crucifixion was only days away and Jesus was trying to prepare the disciples for the events which would soon alter their lives forever. Status-seeking may have been the furthest thing from the mind of Jesus but it was of such great interest to a mother that she apparently interrupted one of Christ's teaching sessions. Her request was brief but bold: could her two sons (who also happened to be two of the twelve disciples) be given seats on the left and right of Jesus when his kingdom was finally established?

Had we been present, some of us might have criticized such a blatant grab for power. The other disciples didn't like it—the Bible says they were indignant—but Jesus responded graciously and turned this awkward situation into an opportunity for teaching.

"You do not know what you are asking for," Jesus said, in denying the request. It is God who determines our place in heaven and we shouldn't worry about it. Of course nonbelievers are concerned about having status and authority over people but this is not to be the concern of Christians.

Then Jesus made a remarkable statement which has been called a "Christian revolution; . . . the complete reversal of all the world's standards. A complete new set of values"[13] was introduced by this one sentence:

> Whoever wishes to become great among you shall be your servant, and whoever wishes to be first among you shall be your slave.

John F. Alexander once described a trip to Asia during which he visited many homes.[14] Most of these had servants whose jobs appeared to be the exact opposite of self-fufillment.

Servants do all sorts of unpleasant jobs without being noticed and often without being thanked. At times they feel used and unjustly criticized. They are obedient, faithful, and expected to keep going even when they feel tired, or would like to be doing something else. Sometimes servants even die in the line of duty. Jesus served like that—to the point of death—and expects his followers to have a willingness to do the same (Phil. 2:5–8).

None of this sounds very appealing to the modern mind. At best, we try to find a balance between self-fulfillment and servanthood. But that is not something which Jesus ever did.[15]

Never did Jesus play up to the crowd, accumulate riches, write his memoirs, or work to build a reputation. Instead, he healed the sick (this is what he did immediately after giving his message on servanthood, Matt. 20:29–34), encouraged the downhearted, comforted the grieving, and freely gave his life as "a ransom for many."

Charles R. Swindoll is a dynamic pastor, writer, and radio speaker whose busy ministry was changed by an in-depth study of servanthood. Serving doesn't come naturally, Swindoll observed when he wrote a book on this subject.[16] "Living an unselfish life is an art . . . you don't have to be brilliant or gifted" to develop the art of serving "But you do have to be willing." You must develop a prayerful attitude which constantly says, "Lord, show me . . . teach me . . . help me . . . to serve and to give."[17]

What are the characteristics of a servant? Perhaps the well-known Beatitudes (Matt. 5:3–12) give us the best definition.

1. *The servant is completely dependent upon God.* The "poor in spirit" are not people who deny that they have God-given abilities and gifts. Instead, such people admit their strengths—as well as their weaknesses—but recognize that everything comes from God. It is he who gives health, capabilities, opportunities, and the resources to face life. Recognizing this, servants know that they are helpless, useless, and "poor" without God. So, they depend on him completely and are assured that he will give strength and spiritual riches as he brings us into his heavenly kingdom.

Many Bible scholars have written about the Sermon on the Mount, and most agree that when a person is "poor in spirit" he or she is truly humble. Such people are not conceited or selfish. Instead they consistently pass what has been called a two-part test of humility.[18] First, they have an authentic desire to help others. Second, they are not defensive in the face of criticism. Instead they work on a simple assumption which says, "Since I have nothing to prove, I have nothing to lose."

2. *The servant is deeply concerned about sin.* When we read, "blessed are those who mourn," it is natural to think that this refers only to people who are grieving over a death. But the statement of Jesus is much broader. It implies a deep sorrow over the sin in ourselves and in the world.

Easy believism has stimulated the idea that Christians are to be always "bubbling" with joy and enthusiasm. We all agree that sin is bad, but we also know that God forgives and because of this awareness, we sometimes have very little anguish over sin in our own lives or in the lives of others. If people's innermost thoughts were suddenly made public, we might discover that many of us do not have much inner joy and that many of us secretly admire the blatant sinfulness so common in this world. When we combine a "shallow idea of joy" with this lackadaisical view of sin, the inevitable result is "a superficial kind of person and a very inadequate kind of Christian life."[19]

The true servant is deeply concerned about sin and firmly committed to working against the powerful and destructive suffering which comes because of sin's influence. Servants who have this attitude take sin seriously and only find true comfort and joy in the knowledge that God does forgive and in time will eradicate all sin and sin-produced sadness.

3. *The servant is gentle.* In our language, gentleness and meek-

ness are not highly respected qualities. They imply weakness, a soft wishy-washy attitude, and a spineless unwillingness to stand up for anything. It is ridiculous to think that such people would really "inherit" and have an influence in this world.

The Greek word which is translated "gentle" or "meek" does not mean spineless, however. It means "self-controlled"—able to express oneself with confidence, strength, and conviction. Such people can be angry about sin and strongly critical of injustice, but without giving in to irresponsible condemnation or uncontrolled passion.

William Barclay has argued convincingly that throughout history the people who have been great, have also had the "gift of self-control," and have kept "their passions, and instincts, and impulses under discipline."

> No man can lead others until he has mastered himself; no man can serve others until he has subjected himself; no man can be in control of others until he has learned to control himself. But the man who gives himself into the complete control of God will gain this meekness which will indeed enable him to inherit the earth.[20]

Clearly, such gentleness cannot be "turned on" or developed by an act of self-determination. We must ask God to make us gentle and self-controlled, expecting that his Holy Spirit will bring these servant characteristics into our lives (Gal. 5:22, 23).

4. *The servant has a deep desire to be holy.* Such people realize that true happiness and fulfillment never come to the person who dabbles deliberately in sin, or who is caught up in the pursuit of possessions or the struggle for success and status.

Perhaps many Christians have a concern about spiritual growth and a desire to live lives which please God. Often, however, we do not grow very fast because we have only a half-hearted interest in being delivered from the world's pollution.

The people who really experience spiritual fulfillment are those who have a perpetual desire to know and to please God. They have an insatiable appetite for what is right, an intense drive to see justice done, and a powerful desire to obey God's commands. Such people avoid activities which would be harmful or could dull their spiritual appetites. When self-destructive fantasies and thoughts appear, these are not allowed to occupy the mind but are replaced by thinking which is honorable to God (Phil. 4:8).

All of this goes against human nature. Most of us prefer the passing satisfaction of nonnutritious "junk food" which comes in the form of self-centered ambition and hedonistic pleasure. "Junk foods," as we know, can be habit-forming but they contribute little to real growth and fulfillment. The true Christian servant, instead, hungers and thirsts for what is right and holy.

5. *The servant sincerely cares about others.* Here is an attitude of compassion and a deep desire to help—even when the help is not deserved or appreciated.

Books on counseling often mention the importance of empathy— that ability to understand and "feel with" another person. When a sincere attitude of caring exists, without a trace of aloofness or holier-than-thou pity, the servant is more effective and better able to help.

Have you ever noticed how medical personnel differ? Some doctors and nurses are cold and distant. They may give efficient care, and it may be that the aloofness protects them from a draining overinvolvement in the patient's suffering, but the aloofness conveys a lack of compassion and this can hinder the patient's progress toward recovery.

Charles Swindoll, whom we mentioned earlier, has suggested that true servants show three basic ingredients: a willingness to *give*—freely, anonymously, generously, voluntarily and personally; a willingness to *forgive*—completely, like God has forgiven us; and a willingness to *forget*—by refusing to hold grudges, to keep judging or to think bitter thoughts.[21]

Such attitudes form the essence of "mercy." When we treat others in such a caring way, we begin to discover that others care for us in return.

6. *The servant has pure motives.* I once read about a man who was given a plaque to hang in his office. It was placed where it could be seen whenever he looked up from his desk. The plaque had only three words: WHAT'S YOUR MOTIVE?

It is possible, I suppose, to become so worried about our motives that we spend all of our time in introspection and give almost no effort to serving. Nevertheless, there is great value in examining ourselves (Gal. 6:4) and frequently asking "what's my motive?" What is my real reason for serving on a church committee, writing an article, spending time with my family, or pushing to get ahead at work?

If we are honest, most of us will discover that our motives aren't always pure. They usually will be mixed with some selfishness, desire to manipulate others, and the hypocrisy which Jesus criticized so strongly. The Christian lives in a constant struggle to have motives which are free of selfishness and consistent with God's pure will for our lives.

No one can give rules to help another develop pure motives. With God's help, and sometimes with the help of a good friend, you must decide if it is right to flatter, to avoid criticizing, or to attend social gatherings primarily because these activities will help you get ahead. Ultimately, it is you who determines why you go to church, study, work hard, take part in politics, read a book like this, or get involved in serving others.

When this self-analysis reveals motives which we don't like, we can ask God to change both our inner motives and the resulting outward behavior. Our goal as Christians is to become more and more like Christ—who alone had pure motives. As we read about Christ, and deliberately seek to be like him, our motives get clearer and less clouded by personal ambitions.

7. *The servant is a peacemaker.* It is difficult to be a servant who ministers to the needs of others; it is even harder to bring an end to conflict and a resolution between two warring or disagreeing factions. Perhaps this is the greatest test of a servant's skill.

When Jesus talked about peacemakers he wasn't discussing people who love peace, have peace, or keep the peace. His words implied action—getting involved by our actions and words in an effort to bring about peace.

It has been said that peacemakers are "called the sons of God" because only the child of God has the ability and, often, the desire to bring peace. In working to remove tension and to bring peace, we are "doing a God-like work . . . engaged in the very work which the God of peace is doing (Rom. 15:33; 2 Cor. 13:11; 1 Thess. 5:23; Heb. 13:20). . . The man who divides men is doing the devil's work; the man who unites men is doing God's work."[22]

A peacemaker is the servant who. . . First, is at peace with himself—internally, at ease . . . not agitated, ill-tempered, in turmoil . . . and therefore not abrasive. Second, he/she works hard to settle quarrels, not start them . . . is accepting, tolerant, finds no pleasure in being negative.[23]

As with every other kind of service, peacemaking gets us involved in the lives of others. It is easiest to sit in my own peaceful little room while other people tear one another apart. Instead, I am responsible to leave my own peaceful environment for awhile, and get involved in helping others find peace—with each other, with God, and with themselves. Surely there can be no more worthwhile (or more difficult) calling.

8. *The servant expects persecution.* After giving such a difficult list of goals for the servant, it would have been nice if Jesus had concluded with a promise of happiness and bliss for all who work to develop these traits. Instead, Jesus promises persecution and gives a message which Christians seldom hear today: If you are a servant of Christ, you can expect to be persecuted—just like sincere believers have been persecuted for centuries.

There is a good reason for this opposition. The true servant of Jesus Christ lives a life which is so different and so much at odds with the standards of society that nonbelievers feel uncomfortable, sometimes threatened, and often inclined to condemn. The world expects the rich to be blessed, not the poor. There is admiration for:

—the happy-go-lucky and carefree, not those who take evil so seriously that they mourn over it;
—the strong and brash, not the meek and gentle;
—the full, not the hungry;
—those who mind their own business, not those who meddle in other men's matters and occupy their time in do-goodery like "showing mercy" and "making peace";
—those who attain their ends even if necessary by devious means, not the pure in heart who refuse to compromise their integrity;
—those who are secure and popular, and live at ease, not those who have to suffer persecution.[24]

It is not surprising that the culture of the world and the "counter-culture of Christ are at loggerheads with each other."[25] We may be grateful for the honesty of Jesus in warning us that the servant's role is difficult. We may recognize and take comfort in the fact that God is fully aware of all our persecutions. We may make up our minds to rejoice when trials come and when we are treated unjustly (James 1:2; Matt. 5:12). We may accept the somewhat pious, but nevertheless valid truth that God wants not to make life easy, but to make men and women great.[26] But the fact still remains that loving service is not easy. It is not difficult to understand why many believers prefer a watered-down easy-believism brand of Christianity.

The Art of Transforming Society: Love Extended

Earlier in the twentieth century the church began to develop a sharp division between those who emphasized worship, prayer, personal spiritual development, and evangelism in contrast to others who plunged enthusiastically into social service. The first group was most concerned about condemning sin while the second was more interested in changing society. People in both groups were often sincere and dedicated, but they failed to recognize that there can be no true spirituality without loving compassion, and no real compassion without pure living and a hatred of sin.

As the years passed, love became the rallying cry of both groups but love was defined differently. The religious conservatives emphasized the love of God that sent Christ to die for the sins of the world; the theological liberals used "love" as a rallying cry for social action. In some cases, these social activists denied the existence of a personal God and suggested instead that "God" was just an old-fashioned name for "love."[27]

In the midst of this debate, H. Richard Niebuhr published a significant book[28] in which he analyzed the struggles faced by Christians who serve a God of love and who also are called to be in the world but not really a part of it. For a long time we tried to set "Christ against culture," and at other times we have tried to accommodate and assimilate our beliefs with the world. More biblical, Niebuhr wrote, is a view which sees Christ as "the transformer of culture."

Such a conclusion pulls together some of the old liberal and conservative perspectives. It recognizes that all human beings have fallen into sin and need salvation in Jesus Christ. But in addition to evangelism and discipleship, there is a God-given mandate for Christians to permeate the society and work to bring improvement and change.

The loving believer has a responsibility to:

—work at eliminating poverty, hunger, injustice and war;[29]
—take leadership in preserving the environment from further erosion and decay;[30]

—challenge evil and immorality while, at the same time, working to bring changes;

—resist such modern philosophical idols as humanism, materialism and hedonism; and

—equip ourselves as God's servants who battle the ever-powerful forces of evil which presently exert their destructive influences on the earth (Eph. 6:10–20).

As people whose prime characteristic is love, we must be concerned in practical ways with the redemption of individuals and the care of society around us. We must learn to love God with heart, soul, mind, and strength, knowing that only then can we love our neighbors and ourselves.

Some Conclusions about Giving Love

In the preceding pages, we have considered something of what it means to be a true disciple of Christ who is characterized by "the mark of the Christian"[31]—a clear, visible love.

We have seen that love is far deeper than sexual attraction or the sentimentality of popular ballads.

We have seen that the person who really loves is a servant, and we have considered how servanthood is much more demanding than we might assume.

We have seen that love must not stop at the door of our homes or on the steps of our churches. Christian love must spill into the culture, transforming it even if some people resist.

Two concluding comments remain.

First, we must never get the idea that the loving servant is a doormat who gets pushed around and who never expresses anger over injustice or resistance to sin. To be a servant is not to squelch our drives, to forget about setting high goals or to be satisfied with the mediocre. Pure love is gracious and sensitive to other people, but it stands up for what is right and does not reject excellence. Instead of being weak and powerless, love is potent and motivating—sometimes more so because it is so gentle.

Paul's description of love is familiar but worth reviewing.

Love is very patient and kind
never jealous or envious,
never boastful or proud,
never haughty or selfish or rude.

Love does not demand its own way.
It is not irritable or touchy.
It does not hold grudges and will hardly even notice
when others do it wrong.
It is never glad about injustice,
but rejoices whenever truth wins out.
If you love someone you will be loyal to him no matter
what the cost.
You will always believe in him,
and always stand your ground in defending him (1 Cor. 13:4–7, LB).

Is it surprising that the apostle adds that we should let love be our greatest aim (1 Cor. 14:1)?

This brings us to our second concluding observation. Love is not something to be practiced alone.

Without Christ, there would be no *source* of our love. It is only because of his love to us that we in turn can love others (1 John 4:19).

Without others, there would be no *recipients* of our love. We don't just "love" in a vacuum. We love something or some person. We also love along with others.

Without others, there would be no *sharing* of our love. In our "rugged individualism" mentality we have tended to think of loving service, spiritual growing, worshiping, and evangelizing as something which individuals do, each one alone. We have put so much emphasis on personal holiness, personal devotions, and personal witnessing that we have almost forgotten that God has placed us in communities of believers.

When Jesus announced that the mark of a Christian is love, he was talking to a group of disciples. Later biblical writers emphasized the importance of serving, helping, encouraging, and loving one another. We are instructed to be "doing good" both to each other and, as a group, to "all men" in the world around us (Gal. 6:10).

The giving love which characterizes individual believers becomes stronger and more powerful when it characterizes and flows through groups of Christians. Others should be able to see that Christians have homes and churches that are dominated not by conflict but by a giving, Christian love.

Flee immorality. . . . Your body is a
temple of the Holy Spirit who is in
you. . . . For you have been bought
with a price; therefore glorify God in
your body.

1 Corinthians 6:18–20

The Lord knows how to rescue the
godly from temptation.

2 Peter 2:9

8
Sanctified Sex

Puritans don't have a very good reputation in our period of history. We tend to think that these sixteenth and seventeenth-century Christians were uptight, rigid, pleasure-denying individuals who, above all, were prudish and opposed to sex. The modern "Playboy philosophy" has been described by one of its advocates as a "rebellion against Puritanism" and against "Puritan hang-ups."[1] Even people who don't read *Playboy* magazine use the word "Puritan" to describe those who are sexually inhibited and theologically narrow. Few words in the English language are more derisive than "Puritan."

Puritans, however, were not as inhibited and opposed to sex as many of their modern critics claim. Apparently, many of these people were "young, fierce, progressive intellectuals, very fashionable and up-to-date." In contrast to many church leaders at the time who praised celibacy and frowned on sexual intercourse even within marriage, the Puritans declared that the sex drive was good because it was created by God. There was general acceptance of the idea that sex between a husband and wife should be pleasurable. This view so shocked the clergy in that era that many must have agreed when

Thomas More charged that Puritans "lust fast in their lechery" and are characterized by "sensual and licentious living."

In spite of their bad image, especially among people today, might it be true that the Puritans really had a healthy Christian view about sex?

Those believers were first called Puritans because they wanted to purify the church by sweeping away medieval theology and tradition-encrusted forms of worship. The Puritans wanted a return to biblical Christianity and that included—but was not limited to—a conformity to the Bible's teaching about sex.

Catholic tradition at that time praised celibacy and tended to look down on marriage. Sexual intercourse between a husband and wife was tolerated, but only for the purpose of creating children. In contrast, the Puritans exalted marriage, criticized the idea that celibacy is a virtue, and agreed with Calvin that "conjugal intercourse is a thing that is pure, honorable and holy because it is a pure institution of God."

Consistent with this high view of sex within marriage was the belief that sex was a private and sacred experience which was not to be flaunted or treated lightly. The Puritans did have taboos against sexual perversions including adultery, lechery, and overt homosexuality. The taboos and rules about sex were not made because the Puritans thought that sex and pleasure were wrong or unchristian. The rules were designed to help believers conform to the guidelines set forth in the Bible.

Puritans were not prudes, observes Leland Ryken.

> The Puritan ideal of sexual love between husband and wife arose as a reaction against an excessively negative attitude toward sex. Today the Puritan ideal stands as a corrective to the opposite extreme of total permissiveness and unbridled lust. Divorced from its context of love and armed with the seductive idea that it is wrong to restrain one's natural impulses, sex has become a cultural obsession. The obsession has not brought freedom but bondage—bondage to sexual appetite, perversion, and the tendency to look upon people as sex objects.[2]

Like the Puritans, many contemporary Christians would accept the conclusion that God has created us with sexual desires and that loving sex within marriage is desirable, honorable, and intended to be pleasurable. Many would agree with the couple who prayed, "Lord, help us to think of sex as you first thought of it, a gift to celebrate, excellent in every way."[3] Some might even agree with the conclusion that "Christians should be sexier than anyone," because "sex at its best is a spiritual union between a man and a woman and the Lord."[4] When we come down to the realities of everyday living, however, I suspect that most people, including Christians, find that their sexual urges and attitudes leave them more with frustrations and futility, than with excitement and enthusiasm. Sexual intercourse apart from marriage, overt homosexuality, pornography on the newsstands and television screens—these have become a part of our way of life. Explicit, titillating references to self-gratifying sex permeate the media, dominate modern advertising, and are heard in classrooms, in casual conversation and sometimes even in sermons. Surely it *is* true that while they proclaim their sexual freedom, many Westerners have become slaves to their sexual urges. It is almost impossible to live in our culture and remain uninfluenced by the perverted sexual obsessions of our era. Even those modern Puritans who want to avoid sexual sin and to "celebrate their sexuality" in accordance with biblical principles, often find that they are controlled by lust, and bored in bed. Perhaps it isn't surprising that so many people apparently conclude that purity is impossible in a sex-saturated society such as ours.

A Question about Sexual Purity

Some have blamed Sigmund Freud for giving people the idea that psychologists are especially interested in sex and experts in understanding perversions. Whether or not this is true (I don't think it is), it seems that many conference planners and church leaders feel that a Christian psychologist is the person best qualified to speak on sex.

When I have accepted such speaking invitations, I have pointed to the Bible's approval of sexual intercourse within marriage (see, for example, 1 Cor. 7:2–5 and Heb. 13:4) and have referred to the strong scriptural warnings against lust and sex apart from marriage (Eph. 5:3–7; Col. 3:5, 6; 1 Cor. 6:16–20). Those who speak and write about sex usually acknowledge that control is difficult and try to give practical guidelines to help people avoid sexual sin. Many of these guidelines are both biblical and helpful:

• Recognize that almost everyone struggles with sexual frustrations.
• If you are overwhelmed by sexual pressures, don't accept the idea that things will never be better.

- Get into the habit of praying about your sexuality—asking for God's help with self-control and fulfillment.
- Avoid pornography and other sexually stimulating materials.
- If you are married, learn to talk with your mate about your sexual needs and frustrations, and get some help through books[5] or counseling if you continue to be unfulfilled.
- Remember that God understands and forgives when we confess our sins.

Behind these and other suggestions for sexual control or fulfillment there exists a more basic question which believers and sex counselors tend to overlook: why should we bother to live in accordance with biblical standards of sexual behavior?

All around us, people have reduced sex to a physiological "high" in which both parties enjoy a self-centered relationship. With the possible exception of sex between adults and children, almost any form of sexual involvement is accepted by at least some segment of our society. Following a slow process, some of us move from shock and outrage about the country's declining morals; through a time of thinking that "the situation is bad but not surprising"; and on to the view that "perhaps such behavior really isn't as bad as I once thought."

Psychologists might call this process "habituation"—a gradual dulling of our sense of outrage and a slow acceptance of the society's degenerating moral standards. Some Christians who once were shocked at reports of marital infidelity, divorce, premarital sex, and overt homosexuality—to name a few—now regard these practices as inevitable, especially among young people. At times the biblical standards of sexuality are overlooked or explained away. Perhaps it isn't surprising that some people aren't interested in self-control and a sanctified (set apart) sexuality. They have fallen into a philosophy which claims to honor Christ but in practice worships hedonism. It is a form of easy believism accepted by even sincere believers who apparently have never thought seriously about the question of why we should bother with sexual purity.

The Basis of Sexual Purity

Like "Puritanism," "holiness" is a misunderstood and discredited word which we often avoid, especially when speaking about ourselves. Nevertheless, we cannot avoid the clear biblical teaching that Christians are to be holy, as we discussed in a previous chapter. This doesn't mean that we will be perfect in this life, but through the influence of the Holy Spirit (2 Thess. 2:13; 1 Peter 1:2) willing Christians can become more and more pure, spiritually mature, and Christlike. This leads to something more than the ethical respectability and seeming godliness (2 Tim. 3:5) which is seen in many nonbelievers and stagnant Christians. In contrast, true holiness comes from God alone through the power of the Holy Spirit. It is likely to arouse resistance from the people who observe it, and it sometimes brings persecution from others (2 Tim. 3:12).

The emphasis on Christian holiness is seen with special clarity in the book of 1 Peter where the writer instructs us to:

> Prepare your minds for action; be self-controlled; set your hope fully on the grace to be given you when Jesus Christ is revealed. As obedient children, do not conform to the evil desires you had when you lived in ignorance. But just as he who called you is holy, so be holy in all you do, for it is written: "Be holy, because I am holy. . . ."
>
> Dear friends, I urge you, as foreigners and strangers in the world, to abstain from sinful desires, which war against your soul. Live such good lives among the pagans that though they accuse you of doing wrong, they may see your good deeds and glorify God (1 Peter 1:13–16; 2:11, 12, NIV).

This emphasis on holy living leads us to three biblical conclusions which help us answer the question of why we should bother to live sexually pure lives.

The Holiness of God. Although our lips proclaim otherwise, most of us have a view of God which, in the words of J. B. Phillips, is much too small. We may be offended when television comedians flippantly refer to God as "the man upstairs" but few of us even begin to think of God as he was viewed by the biblical saints.

It is true, perhaps, that some of these spiritual giants—especially in Old Testament times—had a limited understanding of God's love and mercy. Some of their awe was mixed with fear and terror. Even in New Testament times, God's absolute power and flawless perfection were accepted without question. Near the end of his life, for example, when John saw the vision which is recorded in the last book of the Bible, the apostle fell on his face "as a dead man" as he came into the presence of God and heard the heavenly choirs singing "Holy, Holy, Holy, is the Lord God Almighty."

In the opening sentence of his massive *Institutes of the Christian*

Religion, John Calvin writes that "true and solid wisdom consists almost entirely of two parts: the knowledge of God and of ourselves."[6] This knowledge of God and of ourselves are bound together, according to Calvin. "Man never attains to a true self-knowledge until he has previously contemplated the face of God and come down after such contemplation to look at himself."[7]

How does this relate to our sexual attitudes? When we ignore God's true nature, our thinking and self-understanding is distorted. We begin to see ourselves and our own standards as being the final and absolute authority.

> Since nothing appears within us or around us that is not tainted with very great impurity, so long as we keep our mind within the confines of human pollution, anything which is in some small degree less defiled, delights us as if it were most pure.[8]

To avoid such distorted thinking, we must constantly be reminding ourselves about what God is like. It is not simplistic to conclude that the best way to maintain sexual purity is to ponder the characteristics of God. We can see these divine attributes on almost every page of the Bible. They are listed repeatedly in the Psalms and spelled out clearly in books like A. W. Tozer's powerful volume, *The Knowledge of the Holy.*[9] When we really begin to comprehend what God is like, we become less inclined to displease and grieve him by sinning. Sin is always against God (Ps. 51:4) and it brings both divine sadness and, in time, painful consequences for the one who refuses to repent.

The Destructive Nature of Sin. Like "holiness," the idea of sin is not taken very seriously by many people today. Instead of something to be confessed and forgiven, sin is more often seen as a harmless self-indulgence to be laughed at and tolerated. Millions of people devour the titillating memoirs of sexually loose celebrities and watch sexually explicit scenes in movies, television dramas, and stage plays. Rarely does anyone call such behavior "sin," and those who do so can expect ridicule, criticism, charges of being "closed minded" or the admonition to "mind your own business."

One of the reasons why we take sin so lightly is that we fail to see its devastating power. Tozer has observed that "until we see ourselves as God sees us, we are not likely to be much disturbed over conditions around us as long as they do not get so far out of hand as to threaten our comfortable way of life. We have learned to live with unholiness and have come to look upon it as the natural and expected thing."[10]

When the New Testament describes sin in human beings it often uses the term "flesh."[11] Clearly this involves something deeper than isolated acts of disobedience or self-indulgence. The flesh according to the apostle Paul (Gal. 5:19–21; Col. 3:5–9), refers to our fallen nature and is expressed in such powerful deeds and inner attitudes as "immorality, impurity, sensuality, idolatry, sorcery, enmities, strife, jealousy, anger, disputes, dissensions, factions, envyings, drunkenness, carousings, and things like these." Augustine concluded that all of this could be reduced to two main categories: *pride* (self-aggrandizement) and *sensuality* (self-indulgence). Luther concluded that the root of all fleshly activity was *unbelief,* and more recent writers have noted that anxiety, egoism, and deep self-loathing are at the basis of fleshly lust.

Whatever may be our conclusions about the exact meaning of "the flesh," it is clear that God cannot tolerate or even look at fleshly acts of sin. Although he forgives sin (1 John 1:9)—that is the "good news" of the gospel—he also hates it and, because of the death of Jesus Christ we know that sin will someday be gone from the earth.

In the meantime we must reject the notion that sin, including sexual impurity, is something cute and harmless. In an attempt to avoid the word "sin" we have invented other terms which are less judgmental and more acceptable. Instead of words like "profanity," "permissiveness," "perversion" or "pornography" we talk about "freedom of speech," "sexual freedom," "alternate life styles," and "sexual realism."[12] But all of this is still sin, in God's sight, and sin of all kinds is indescribably powerful and destructive. The Bible warns against it in the most ominous terms (eg: Gal. 5:21; Eph. 5:3–7). If, with God's help, we could understand and appreciate the power of sin, we would be less inclined to indulge in our fleshly desires or to find reasons to justify our immorality.

The Power of Satan. In the preface to his famous *Screwtape Letters,*[13] C. S. Lewis noted that there are two errors which creep into our thinking about devils. One is to disbelieve in their existence. The other is to believe and to have an excessive interest in them. The devils themselves, Lewis concluded, "are equally pleased by both errors."

A similar conclusion might be reached about the prince of all devils—Satan himself. He masquerades as an angel of light and goodness (2 Cor. 11:13–15) but underneath this attractive exterior is a creature who really is a liar and deceiver (Rev. 12:9), as vicious as a roaring lion prowling around looking for someone to devour (1 Peter 5:8).

Several years ago, a popular television comedian frequently joked about his sins while an amused audience responded with hearty laughter whenever they heard these familiar words: "The devil made me do it!" While some people blame their sexual sins on the devil, and thus keep from admitting their own responsibility, others don't even believe that the devil exists. Surely the devil himself would be equally pleased with both of these conclusions.

In contrast, the Bible tells us to "be on the alert" against Satan and his demonic assistants (1 Peter 5:8). We are to "resist the devil" (James 4:7; 1 Peter 5:9), not by trying to squelch him in our own strength, but by protecting ourselves with "the full armor of God" (Eph. 6:11). This includes faith, prayer, obedience to God, knowledge of God's Word, and the power which comes from the Holy Spirit who lives inside believers and who alone can overcome satanic forces (Eph. 6:11–18; James 4:7, 8; 1 John 4:4).

The New Testament seems to assume that believers would not be ignorant of Satan's tactics (2 Cor. 2:11), but many of us hardly give the devil a thought. We are like soldiers on a battlefield who rarely pay any attention to the enemy and who almost never think about the tactics of the opposition. It isn't surprising that we so often fall into sexual and other sins. Instead of living a victorious Christian life, we limp along as spiritually wounded casualties who, even in defeat, may not realize that we are still at war.

Drawing on the teachings of Scripture, Richard Lovelace[14] has identified five common strategies of Satan. To be aware of these is an important step in resisting them.

Temptation. This may involve luring people into serious acts of sin, but the devil also entices us into accepting attitudes and outlooks which go against biblical teaching. Without giving this much thought we begin to think in ways which excuse or justify sin.

People who have been on a diet know some of the subtle ways by which we talk ourselves into eating the high-calorie items that we are supposed to avoid. "Everybody's doing it," we conclude as we watch others eat. "Just this once won't hurt." "Nobody will know." "To partake will be a pleasant experience." "We can go back on the diet tomorrow."

Satan surely raises similar excuses to lure us into sinful acts and thoughts. "Surely nothing is wrong with it," he urges. "It will be good for you to know how others live." "God will forgive, so why not give in?" "This is a special occasion so why don't you drop your guard?"

These ideas slip into our minds and contain such a subtle mixture of truth and error that we often give in. Every time we yield, it gets easier the next time temptations slip into our thinking.

Deception. Satan is a liar whose ability to deceive is so good that even believers are fooled (2 Cor. 4:4). We must be on the alert, therefore, constantly asking if what we are hearing or thinking is really right and consistent with biblical teaching.

Physical attack. Sometimes Satan's forces pull us down physically and bring on psychological problems such as discouragement or hopelessness.

Accusation. In the Old Testament, Satan came into the presence of God and pointed out the supposed weak points of Job. Today, the devil tells God about our failures (Rev. 12:10). It seems likely that he also causes Christians to be critical of one another, and leads nonbelievers into an awareness of our greatest faults. Even worse, perhaps, "satanic forces attack Christians directly in their own minds with disturbingly accurate accounts of their faults, seeking to discourage those who are most eager and able to work for the kingdom."[15]

Possession. Christians are divided today over the question of whether and how demonic forces can control an individual. In Bible times demonic possession was clearly evident and it would be difficult to prove that this one satanic activity has been stopped in our period of history.

At this point we might remember again that to deny Satanic activity would be wrong, but it is equally wrong to be overwhelmed and overfascinated by the devil's deceptive devices. The believer who is "on the alert" and determined to stand against the devil can rest assured that when we submit to God and resist Satan, the devil will flee. The Bible promises this (James 4:7) and Satan himself knows that the Holy Spirit in us is greater than the devil who is in this world (1 John 4:4). It *is* possible to resist the temptations to fall into sexual sin.

For the person who wants to experience sexual fulfillment in accordance with biblical standards, it can be helpful to understand doctrinal truths and it can be useful to set up some rules about what we should and should not do. Doctrinal propositions and rules alone are not sufficient, however, without the presence and power of the Holy Spirit.

It is true, as one writer has noted, that our permissive and sex-saturated society exerts a tremendous pressure on people of all ages, of both sexes (but especially males), both nonbelievers and Christians.

Preying on the strong sex drives of boys and men, the pornographic picture, book, or movie teases men to seek sexual pleasures forbidden by God because of their destructiveness to the personality, the marriage union, and the stability of society.

I offer no excuses for the husband who gives in to these temptations, sacrificing his marriage and his family on Satan's altar of sexual indulgence. But of this I am thoroughly convinced: apart from a spiritual rebirth and a life committed to the control of the indwelling Holy Spirit, no man is likely to withstand for very long the continuous assault being made against his sexual morality by the devil and his antifamily allies.[16]

The Mind and Sexual Purity

Books and articles on human sexuality and on the problems of living with unfulfilled desires[17] frequently make reference to the mind. It has been suggested that the mind is the "biggest and most powerful sex organ," and that there is little hope for sexual control in the person who does not control his or her thinking.

Social pressures often keep us from acting in ways that are immoral or antisocial. The fear of getting caught or of ruining one's reputation at times keeps all of us from yielding to various temptations. It is easier to keep "on the straight and narrow way" when we are surrounded by people who expect us not to sin. Let two teenagers get alone in a car, however, or let a businessman encounter temptation when he is away from home, and the social restraints are much weaker.

Within our minds there often are no restraints at all. No one (except God) knows our thoughts and it is possible to sit in a classroom, a business meeting, a restaurant or even in church and let our eyes dart around the room, looking for sexually attractive people who become the object of fantasy both then and later. People, including Christians, who wouldn't think of undressing a stranger or any other human being (apart from one's spouse), undress people mentally and sometimes indulge themselves—all in the mind—without apparent guilt. Overt sin is pleasurable. If this were not true we wouldn't be tempted. Mental sin is also enjoyable and at first it is a lot less risky because we can do what we want mentally and no other human being will condemn or know anything about what we are thinking.

Long before psychologists started writing about fantasy, however, Jesus warned of the dangers of mental adultery (Matt. 5:27, 28). Apart from the fact that this can be destructive in itself, such mental sex can make us more vulnerable when opportunities for immoral sexual actions present themselves. We would be much more victorious in resisting such temptations "if we realized that there is much more to temptation than the overt, momentary solicitation to evil." Our strength or weakness at such times "is based on attitudes that have been forming for weeks, months, or even years prior."[18]

It is difficult enough to rid our minds of sensuous mental images, but within recent years psychologists and advertisers have become increasingly alert to something called "subliminal perception."[19] Although this seems less dangerous now than we once feared, it appears nevertheless that our minds can be "massaged" and subtly molded by the constant bombardment of messages from television, radio, written publications, music lyrics, and the people with whom we interact. Our conscious minds can evaluate and discern the ideas that we hear, but when values and attitudes hit us repeatedly at a subconscious level, they get a foothold which, at first, we may not even recognize.

In an insightful article, D. G. Kehl has suggested that if:

> Satan cannot overtly *corrupt* our minds (2 Cor. 11:3) or *defile* them (Titus 1:15) or *blind* them (2 Cor. 4:4) or *confuse* them (2 Thess. 2:2) or *unsettle* them (Luke 12:29) or *divert* them (James 1:8, 4:8) or *discourage* them (Heb. 12:3), he seeks to *bypass* our conscious minds, subtly appealing instead to the intuitive, the irrational, the merely emotional. . . . Satan, the author of imbalance and disharmony is responsible for the current pendulum swing away from God-ordained reason toward a mindless emotionalism, from thought to touchy-feely sensation, from the reasonableness of sound doctrine to the intuition of visionary experience.[20]

When Paul wrote his letter to the Romans, he admonished the believers "to give your bodies as a living sacrifice, consecrated to him and acceptable by him. Don't let the world around you squeeze you into its mold, but let God re-make your minds from within, so that you may prove in practice that the plan of God for you is good, meets all his demands and moves towards the goal of true maturity" (Rom. 12:12, Phillips).

Our bodies, including our minds and sexual actions, are more likely to be "acceptable" to God when we remember and practice two basic ideas.

First, we must avoid destructive thinking. This involves giving attention to what we *take in* to our minds and what we *dwell* on in our thinking.

Several times in this chapter we have mentioned the harmful influence of sexual stimuli. Books, magazines, pictures, movies, and even casual conversation of a sexually explicit nature can poison our thinking and impede our maturation as Christians.

Only a few miles from where we live, there are several "adult X-rated bookstores." The signs in front of these businesses advertise "mature" books and movies, but the truth is just the opposite. Pornography is geared to the sexually and psychologically immature. When we let our minds feast on such materials, when we let our eyes wander around a room looking for sexually arousing people, and even when we linger over sex-oriented advertisements in magazines and newspapers, we are "taking in" ideas which can hinder spiritual growth. It is difficult to cut off the subliminal influences, but we can avoid the blatantly sexual influences and try to avoid those places, publications and sources of music where more subtle sexual stimulation is likely to be present.

In this society, however, it is impossible to avoid sexual influences completely and, since God created sex, it isn't even desirable or healthy to suppress all sexual feelings. It is possible to admire the body and physical characteristics of another human, however, without fantasizing about sexual immorality. The Bible teaches that our minds should dwell on things which are honorable, right, pure, lovely, and excellent (Phil. 4:8). This is far different from the mind which is influenced by a sexual sight or thought and then dwells on that which is lustful, lewd, and self-centered. We can't always control what comes into our minds but, with God's help, we can control what we continue to think about.

Second, we must let God remold our minds. It has been truly stated that the Christian's victory over seduction lies in the indwelling Word of God and the indwelling Spirit of God. "Let God remold your minds from within," the Scriptures state, and then our actions ("practice") will conform to his will and we will move more smoothly "toward the goal of true maturity" (Rom. 12:2, Phillips).

We Christians sometimes get tired about hearing how we must immerse ourselves in the Word of God so that we can understand the Scriptures with increasing clarity. Such warnings need to be repeated, however, because they are so often accepted intellectually but forgotten in practice. By ignoring the Scriptures or giving them only passing attention, we are cut off from the one anchor of stability in this society and we are more likely to be swamped in the storms of sensuality which thunder around us.

Reading the Scriptures and attempting to apply them, however, can become a frustrating exercise if we try to do this in our own strength. The Holy Spirit lives within each believer, to guide and teach us. He helps us understand Scripture, think honorable thoughts, attain fulfillment in this life, and avoid the devastating influences of both conscious and subliminal sexual stimulation.

One psychologist has suggested that within our recent history we have come to a time when saying "no" is out of fashion.[21] "When I say no, I feel guilty," the author of a best-selling book proclaimed,[22] and many people seem to agree that it is cowardly and disruptive to resist the urges of the society in which we live.

But such a conclusion is not new and neither is our era unique. Individuals have always found it easier to go along with the crowd and nowhere is this more apparent than in our slow but quiet acceptance of sexual mores. To take a stand for what we believe and for what the Bible teaches may put us out of step with the drumbeat of society, but by taking such a stand we develop both moral strength and personal identity.[23] We also find ourselves moving in the direction of a sanctified sexuality which ultimately is most fulfilling.

Anyone who won't care for his own
relatives when they need help, especially those living in his own family,
has no right to say he is a Christian.
Such a person is worse than the
heathen.

1 Timothy 5:8 (LB)

I have no greater joy than this, to hear
of my children walking in the truth.

3 John 4

9

Changed Home Life

The family is changing—at least in America.

Almost everyone recognizes this, and most would agree that
some of the changes are good. Other trends are disturbing, however, and in an attempt to discover exactly what is happening to
modern families, the senior editor of a leading magazine recently
went on a fact-finding trip. He interviewed family life experts,
college professors, students, single parents, people living in communes, and family members who lived in more traditional settings.
He talked with children, teens, grandparents, and psychologists.
Then he returned home and wrote a report of his observations.

The family is still very much alive, the editor concluded, but it is
under heavy attack and tremendous pressure. It is involved in a war
"waged in the press, on TV, and on lecture platforms. It is waged
by angry women's libbers, by counselors on the fringes of the
encounter group movement, by student leaders and by college professors." While some respected experts predict that "the traditional
family will make a comeback,"[1] others have observed that publishers and editors are rushing to print books which predict that the
family, as we know it, is finished.

Such uncertainty leaves many people uncomfortable and sometimes frightened. They see marriages breaking up—including long-term marriages, clergy marriages, and the marriages of lay church leaders. Relationships appear to be collapsing all around us and we don't know how to help ourselves. "I have only been married for one year," a young pastor confided recently. "My marriage seems to be in good shape but what can I do to be sure that we won't end up in divorce court? Will my Christianity really make any difference?"

As Christians we are inclined to cry out, "Yes! Christianity *will* make a difference in our homes." Inside, however, many of us realize that the same tension and instability which neighborhood families face, also characterizes Christian homes. Church leaders are discovering that their Christianity does not always prevent or ease family pressure. Something clearly is wrong when the *Christian* family is in trouble!

Some Family Changes

Several years ago, the Gallup Organization conducted a survey of attitudes toward families. The poll discovered that for millions of people, the family—despite all its problems—stands out as life's greatest source of personal satisfaction. Nine out of ten Americans are satisfied or "mostly satisfied" with family life. "Any belief that Americans do not place top priority on the family and family life is completely refuted by the results of this survey," concluded George Gallup. "The findings represent a ringing endorsement of the importance of the family in American life."[2]

In spite of this positive endorsement, however, nearly half of the people questioned felt that family life had deteriorated during the past fifteen years. Many people were apprehensive about the future and most recognized that the family is undergoing some dramatic changes—at least in the United States and Canada.

Family size is getting smaller. The era of big families has passed. While some people may be concerned about overpopulation and the need to restrict family size because of world hunger, most Western couples probably have smaller families because it is fashionable, more convenient, and cheaper to have fewer children. With fewer children, parents should be able to have closer contact with their sons and daughters but there is little evidence to indicate that this is happening. On the contrary, because of economic pressures and the desire for personal fulfillment, increasing numbers of households have both parents working away from home during the day, or with little time for the children on weekends.

Family size is getting smaller. The era of big families has passed. While some people may be concerned about overpopulation and the need to restrict family size because of world hunger, most Western couples probably have smaller families because it is fashionable, more convenient, and cheaper to have fewer children. With fewer children, parents should be able to have closer contact with their sons and daughters but there is little evidence to indicate that this is happening. On the contrary, because of economic pressures and the desire for personal fulfillment, increasing numbers of households have both parents working away from home during the day, or with little time for the children on weekends.

Perhaps more of America was like this at one time in the past, but things are different now. Automobiles, the increased ease of travel, and a mindset which encourages us to move frequently have all contributed to the scattering of families. Education—including sex education and religious instruction—has been taken over by the schools; most people leave the family every day to "go to work"; and entertainment has shifted away from the "parlor games" which emphasized togetherness toward increasing dependence on television and other forms of diversion. With the high cost of housing, most of us cannot afford to keep aged family members in the home, and even if they have the space, many families lack the patience, resources, or time to care for needy relatives.

Family commitment appears to be getting weaker. Family life experts frequently cite the study which showed that the average father in one community spent only thirty-seven seconds a day with his young children![4] Even if this figure is inaccurate, we do know that children perceive such absences as rejection, and rejection in turn breeds resentment and hostility.[5]

I have a friend[6] who has concluded that our entire society is moving toward a belief that commitment to anything—including commitment to the family—is becoming more and more rare. We move into careers, religions, dating relationships, and marriages determined to "try things out for a while," and convinced that we can always move into something else if we sense the need for a change. As a result of this attitude, we are less willing to commit ourselves to careers or to families and less inclined to persist in working through problems whenever difficulties arise.

In its wake, this attitude leaves broken marriages, half-finished projects, and uncompleted academic programs. It also leaves guilt, self-condemnation, and despair in innumerable people who reach their 30s and 40s having accomplished little in life and still searching for direction, purpose, and life stability.

To these family changes, we could add mention of the apparent increase in illegitimacy, abortion, homosexuality, spouse-beating, child abuse, and mistreatment of older parents. We also could discuss what one committee of experts has called the "four basic ways in which American families and households are different now from what they were in the 1950s": there has been a significant rise in the number of single person households; the elderly are comprising a larger part of the population; there is an increase in single-parent families; and there has been a dramatic increase in the percentage of married women who have joined the labor force.[7] Equally thought-provoking, perhaps, is the observation of Dr. Urie Bronfenbrenner, a highly regarded Cornell psychologist who wrote about "forces of disorganization" in the family. The quotation is worth reading carefully.

Studies of human behavior have yielded few generalizations that are firmly grounded in research and broadly accepted by specialists, but there are two . . . that do meet these exacting criteria.

1. Over the past three decades literally thousands of investigations have been conducted to identify the developmental antecedents of behavior disorders and social pathology. The results point to an almost omnipresent overriding factor: family disorganization.

2. Much of the same research also shows that the forces of disorganization arise primarily not from within the family but from the circumstances in which the family finds itself and from the way of life that is imposed on it by those circumstances.

Specifically, when those circumstances and the way of life they generate undermine relationships of trust and emotional security between family members, when they make it difficult for parents to care for, educate, and enjoy their children, when there is no support or recognition from the outside world for one's role as a parent and when time spent with one's family means frustration of career, personal fulfillment, and peace of mind, then development of the child is adversely affected. The first symptoms are emotional and motivational: disaffection, indifference, irresponsibility, and inability to follow through in activities requiring application and persistence. In less favorable family circumstances the reaction takes the form of antisocial acts injurious to the child and society. Finally, for children who come from environments in which the capacity of the family to function has been most severely traumatized by such destructive forces as poverty, ill health, and discrimination, the consequences for the child are seen not only in the spheres of emotional and social maladjustment but also in the impairment of the most distinctive of human capacities: the ability to think, to deal with concepts and numbers at even the most elementary level.[8]

This sobering analysis brings us back to the question which was raised earlier. Can Christianity really make any difference in my family?

Some Family Stresses

Literally thousands of books, articles, family-life workshops, and enrichment seminars have attempted to analyze family problems and suggest solutions for improving the home. I am left with the uneasy feeling, however, that much of this effort isn't making a great difference. Is it possible that some Christian communicators are covering deep family wounds with little bandages of advice and encouragement? Do many of us attend the seminars and read the family books, but make no effort to change our family relationships—even when the advice we get is helpful? Have we all become experts in diagnosing the sources of family stress, but impotent in bringing about cures because so many of us are unwilling or unable to change our family life styles?

Like the physician who diagnoses an illness and then intervenes to bring healing, we must become aware of our own family stresses and then get involved in working on the changes that will bring improvement to our homes. Three areas of family stresses hold a special concern for Christians.

Community pressures. Some writers have argued persuasively that the family is under deliberate attack. This attack comes both from people who believe in the principles of atheistic humanism and see the family as outdated, and from those whose self-centered values lead them to advocate a collapse of the family and the freeing of women, men, and children to "achieve their unique, individual, full potential."[9]

Christians differ, no doubt, in the extent to which they see such attacks as being real or powerful. Most would agree, however, that the everyday stresses of modern living put family members under pressure, and perhaps the most influential and insidious pressure of all comes from the media, especially television. Attacking television has become a popular pastime and I am reluctant to jump on the anti-TV bandwagon. Nevertheless, I tend to agree with the writer who concluded that television may be a bigger peril than nuclear weapons:

> The bomb is less of a menace because its danger is clearly recognizable, and it is under control. . .
> The menace of television is not clearly recognized, and television is out of control. The physical means of transmitting television—the air waves—are a national asset, but we have turned this asset over to business people whose objective is to make money. . . .
> TV is a sinister danger because its effects are hard to measure. No hood is going to tell an interviewer he is antisocial because he watched television. Few people are going to say they are dull and bland because they spend their evenings watching situation comedies instead of reading or taking night school courses, or that they are flabby because they watch golf instead of playing it.
> The only antidote to the poison of television is to not watch it.[10]

Few people choose this alternative and it is even more difficult to resist the antifamily values which television both reflects and encourages. Here, as with every other temptation, a good defense is to be alert and aware of the dangers (1 Cor 16:13; 1 Thess. 5:6). It is difficult to resist pressures when we know about them; it is impossible to resist if our minds are unaware or unconcerned about the community and media threats to family stability.

Confusion of roles. A sociologist once defined the family as "a small group of people in which one or more adults cares for one or more dependent children."[11] Such a definition may accurately describe some modern families but it is far removed from the Bible's guidelines for family living.

When he created human beings, God made us male and female (Gen. 1:27). He declared that humans were formed in the image of God and throughout the Bible there is never any indication that one sex is inferior to the other. In contrast to Greek, Roman, and even Jewish societies which had a contemptuous attitude toward females, Jesus and his followers elevated women to a dignity which they never had known. Unlike the traditionalists of his day, Jesus conversed with women (John 4:27), taught them (Luke 10:39), defended them (John 8:1–11), was sensitive to them (Mark 12:40–

44), and respected them so much that he described them with a term which to that point had only been applied to "good men" (Luke 13:16).[12]

Even as Jesus championed women's rights, so did the early believers and the writers of the New Testament Epistles. Women took a prominent role in the church. They were "fellow-heirs"—with men—of God's grace (1 Peter 3:7), and accepted as complete equals with men (Gal. 3:28).

Males and females, therefore, are equal, but the Bible also declares that they have different responsibilities—especially in relation to the home.

Suppose that two people decide to form a business partnership. Each partner contributes an equal amount of funds, and the profits are shared equally. Let us assume further, however, that one of the partners concentrates on making sales while the other manages the books. These partners are equal, but they have different responsibilities. If one or both of the partners determined to sweep aside the division of labor, take over the other's job, and abandon any work which was unpleasant, there would be chaos in the business.

This picture could illustrate the state of our society. Many women and some men, justly frustrated with the menial tasks and sexually based mistreatment of their sex, have decided to rebel. They have cast aside traditional roles, demanded liberation, and cried that there must be no distinctions between men and women, or between the ways in which boys and girls are raised. The result has been confusion, especially in the minds of young people. Individuals who sincerely want the best for women, as well as for men, are reluctant to advocate distinct male and female roles lest they be labeled "rigid," "insensitive," or, worst of all, "chauvinistic." Many sensitive believers slither past biblical teaching in this area, because they want to avoid criticism, but then wonder why there is so much confusion and hurt in the home and in society.

We are fooling ourselves if we think that God intended males and females to be identical *in roles and responsibilities*. We may not like it, and in this age of liberation we may wish it were otherwise, but the God who created us and knows us best, gave us distinctive (although overlapping) male and female roles. To ignore this is to keep families in tension and continuing deterioration.

Even committed Christians sometimes bypass biblical teaching and go along with the culture because we are both sincerely concerned about equal rights and equally afraid of losing our contact with nonbelievers if we advocate unpopular biblical standards.

Consider, for example, the Bible's teaching about males. Unlike the *Playboy* philosophy which assumes that the most masculine characteristic is unrestrained sexual pleasure, and in contrast to some feminist views which strip men of their uniqueness, the Bible declares that men are to be leaders in their homes (Eph. 5:23). Men have the responsibility of caring for their families (Eph. 5:29), they are to honor women—lest their spiritual lives suffer (1 Peter 3:7), to respect them (1 Tim. 5:1, 2), to live their lives with the same giving love that Christ showed (Eph. 5:25), and to take ultimate responsibility for child discipline, and teaching spiritual instruction (Eph. 6:4).

Surely it is true that one source of weakness in the church and family today is the failure of men to yield to God's call for leadership. We prefer to let women "handle the home" and then we are surprised when women rebel against masculine insensitivity, and the abdication of the responsibilities which God has given to husbands and fathers.

Women also have roles. Physically they tend to be weaker than men (1 Peter 3:7) but this in no way implies that they are inferior or required to stay passively at home with the diapers and dishes. Proverbs 31 shows that the virtuous woman can, if she chooses, be active in the community, developing her potential and using her skills, including her business abilities. Many godly New Testament women were not housewives (Lydia of Philippi and Chloe of Corinth are examples) and, in contrast, there is nothing in Scripture to suggest that men should never do housework. Nevertheless, it appears that women are given the overall responsibility for household duties including acts of kindness and hospitality (1 Tim. 5; Titus 2:3–5). Married women are to be respectful and submissive to their husbands who, in turn, are to love their wives with a Christlike love and to take responsibility for the family's welfare (Eph. 5:22–33).

Paul's letter to Titus is worth reading carefully, not with a "how-can-I-prove-it-wrong" attitude, but with a willingness to yield to its teachings:

> Older men are to be temperate, dignified, sensible, sound in faith, in love, in perseverance.
> Older women likewise are to be reverent in their behavior, not malicious gossips, nor enslaved to much wine, teaching what is good, that they

may encourage the young women to love their husbands, to love their children, to be sensible, pure, workers at home, kind, being subject to their own husbands, that the word of God may not be dishonored.

Likewise, urge the young men to be sensible, in all things show yourself to be an example of good deeds, with purity in doctrine, dignified, sound in speech which is beyond reproach, in order that the opponent may be put to shame, having nothing bad to say about us (Titus 2:2–8).

Notice how the men and women complement each other with these duties. It has been suggested that "according to Genesis 1 and 2, man is not completely man without feminine influence on his development. Likewise, a woman is not completely woman without masculine influence on her development."[13]

This in no way is meant to imply that only married people are complete. The sexes can influence and interact with each other in many ways apart from marriage. But it "is not good for a man to totally steel himself against any feminine perspective."[14] A totally masculine society or a totally feminine society—like a society with no differences in sex roles—would be a violation of God's proclamation at creation.

Communication failure. It might be interesting, although not of much practical value, to guess how many books and articles have been written about communication in the home. In reading these, one gets the impression that many are saying the same things: listen carefully; try to understand each other; avoid emotionally loaded words, ridicule and name calling; try to deal with one issue at a time; state your own position and feelings clearly and without sarcasm or criticism; be tactful, considerate and courteous; try to be patient; and always be kind.

In the heat of argument, when we often feel threatened, angry and hurt, it is not easy to keep such guidelines in mind and it is even harder to put them into practice. We are more inclined to defend ourselves and to "put down" each other with an attitude far removed from the biblical ideal of love.

It is well known that as our emotional temperature rises, there is a corresponding decline in our judgment, intellect, reasonableness, and productivity.[15] In times of tension, therefore, we must do what we can to lower emotional arousal. Withdrawing temporarily, learning to tense and then to relax our muscles (in an effort to reduce overall tension), and praying can all help in the calming down process. Perhaps the ability to control emotions, to listen carefully, and to communicate clearly are among life's most difficult accomplishments—accomplishments which only come completely with the help of God.

Commitment decline. In his famous *Screwtape Letters,*[16] C. S. Lewis brilliantly speculated about the ways by which the devil deceives believers. Even a superficial reading of the Bible shows that Satan is alert, creative, and extremely persuasive in his tactics. We could ponder, for example, how he might undermine Christian families with a plan such as the following:

* Give believers a deep concern about divorce, pornography, teenage rebellion and similar issues;
* Get them busy analyzing family problems, writing about them, attending seminars, and doing counseling;
* Encourage them to get busy in building better communication; *then*
* Instill some subtle, almost unnoticed, inner attitudes which could undermine the family from within.

Most of us have seen some of these attitudes in others, if not in ourselves. Each can signal a declining commitment to the family.

Consider, for example, the *procrastination mentality* which says—by action if not by words—"I'll give time to my family, but not now." This is an attitude which pushes the family aside in favor of other things. There is no deliberate rejection of the family. We recognize and admit that the family will take some of our time and money. We are determined to provide love and nurture, and we are not deliberately shirking our responsibilities. But everyone knows that families can be dull and problem-filled. It takes energy to build good relationships, so the family is left until a more convenient time. Some family members come to see that they are low in priority and they either withdraw into other activities, or they react in ways that will get attention from the individual—perhaps you—who is not taking the family seriously. Neglect of family members—even by those who are busy—is condemned in Scripture. The person who does not actively care for the household when the need arises, is "worse than an unbeliever" (1 Tim. 5:8).

The *success mentality,* which we discussed in chapter 6, assumes that our major goal in life is to be "successful"—as the culture defines success. Often this attitude gets us so involved with a business or ministry that we forget Christ's statement that whoever wishes to become great should be a servant (Matt. 20:26). But how can we serve others, or even serve ourselves if we have neglected such service in the family? Success in the secular or spiritual world will be empty if we are failures at home.

The *envious mentality* may be denied by most family members, but I suspect it subtly disrupts many homes. Cain envied Abel, Joseph's brothers envied their father's favorite son, and these values within families have continued to this day. Instead of rejoicing when family members reach some goal or get acclaim, some relatives are secretly (and sometimes openly) envious, and there is hurt and jealousy behind the smiles of congratulations. Such envy is not limited to brothers and sisters. There are many examples of envy between husband and wife, and even between children and parents. All envy, along with boasting, is condemned in Scripture (Gal. 5:26). It corrupts individual family members and leads to disorder, arrogance, untruthfulness, and evil. This the Bible calls demonic (James 3:13–16). Are you envious of family members? Only God can really bring about a change in your attitude.

The *hostile mentality* involves bitterness, anger and a critical outlook on life. Often we are able to keep this hidden behind a friendly exterior, but at times the hostility spills out in criticism, unkindness, or sudden violence. The Bible is clear in its teaching that inner bitterness leads to all kinds of trouble—including, perhaps, family troubles (Heb. 12:15). Such bitterness cannot be a characteristic of the Spirit-controlled Christian. He or she, instead, is growing in such traits as love, peace, patience, kindness, and self-control (Gal. 5:22, 23). When these are present in a life, they will be seen at home.

The *depressed mentality* pulls down many family members and disrupts family unity. There are volumes of clinical debate about the causes of depression. Physiological factors are often involved and it is far too simplistic to conclude that we get depressed only because of sin, mid-life burnout or disappointment. More often, depression comes when we are grappling with some loss (including loss of a relationship through death or other separation); and it comes when we harbor anger or hurt inside. Depressed people often pull others down and frustrated family members sometimes fail to understand why the depressed person can't "snap out of it" at will.

The *carnal mentality* is primarily a spiritual problem. According to 1 Corinthians 2:14–3:3 this world has three kinds of people: natural people who are nonbelievers, spiritual people who are walking in a close relationship with God, and carnal people who are Christians, but who are spiritually stagnant. Such people are not much involved in Bible study or in prayer. They may attend church but their thoughts and actions are largely secular. The Bible states that these people are "fleshly," characterized by strife and jealousy, and hardly distinguishable from unbelievers. Such individuals lack spiritual power and their families are little better than those of non-Christians. Surely carnality and easy believism are closely related, and both are enemies of family fulfillment.

The *indiscreet mentality* involves an insensitivity to the power of temptations and the harm that comes from the appearance of evil. In this liberated age, it is common for people of the opposite sex to travel together, attend business luncheons together, and work closely on church committees. None of this is wrong, in itself, but such close relationships can and often do lead to intimacies and misunderstandings which can play havoc with a marriage.

Christian marriages and families break up for a variety of reasons,[17] including the tendency for one or both of the spouses to drift apart and to slowly slide into extramarital friendships. In our own minds we need to remember constantly the words of Scripture: "Abstain from every form of evil" (1 Thess. 5:22) and "Let him who thinks he stands take heed lest he fall" (1 Cor. 10:12).

The *threatened mentality* may apply to both sexes, but I suspect it is more often seen in men. We males are reluctant to admit that we have problems or need help. To face our spiritual, personal, and family weaknesses is risky because such an admission might confront us with the need to admit failure and to change. Many of us don't want that. It is easier to remain miserable and seemingly secure than to risk facing issues and making changes which might ultimately improve life but bring some disruption in the process. In the midst of persistent problems it is always wise to ask yourself, "Am I too threatened to change?" What will you do if the answer is "yes"?

Some Family Conclusions

With the avalanche of articles describing family pressures, there has come a host of recommended solutions.[18] Denominational gatherings, professional conventions, scholarly workshops, and numerous church meetings have all proposed answers to our family dilemmas. Some of these solutions are helpful; some are not—but all try to answer the question once raised in the cover story of a national magazine: "Can the family survive today's shocks?"

Most people would agree that the answer is "yes" but survival won't be easy and neither is it easy to develop a family life which is stable and consistent with biblical teachings. This takes understanding, dedication, commitment and an awareness of some practical areas where we can begin to work.

First, *we must submit ourselves to biblical teaching on the family.* It is easy to get frustrated, confused, and even annoyed by the variety of books, seminars and articles on the family. Too often these overlook the Scriptures and focus, instead, on personal experiences, amusing anecdotes, or interesting family-life principles. These may be proposed in all seriousness, but often they fail to help in practical ways.

Several years ago, in an attempt to find more practical and realistic solutions, 2,000 evangelical leaders gathered for a week-long congress on the family. They came from all over North America and from a variety of denominational and theological backgrounds. They listened to speeches, prayed together, participated in discussions, and prepared an "Affirmation of the Family."* This document was designed to be helpful, practical and solidly based on Scripture.

The "Affirmation" is not perfect, but it can provide an important starting place for family members, church leaders, Sunday school classes, and others who want to study and obey biblical teachings on the family.

Such study may bring us to a second conclusion about solving family problems. *We must admit to ourselves that the modern family is changing.*

The "typical family" was once thought to consist of a working father, a homemaker mother, and two or three children, all living together under one roof, sometimes in the company of a faithful family dog. This no longer describes most modern homes. More typical are families where both husband and wife work, where

---

*The complete affirmation, accompanied by a devotional commentary for families to read together, appears in Gary R. Collins, *Family Talk* (Santa Ana: Vision House, 1978).

single persons live with children but without a mate, or where unmarried adults reside alone or together. Many couples decide to marry, but not to have children. Some people join communes; others live in homosexual or "common-law" heterosexual relationships. Some families still are surrounded by relatives—elderly parents, aunts, uncles, children—all in the same house.

Surely we cannot really understand and help families until we recognize this diversity. Such understanding does not mean we condone living relationships which are sinful, but neither should we conclude that "my family is typical—the way all families are or should be." God gave each of us unique abilities and gifts. We have such a variety of past experiences and differing personalities that even within the biblical guidelines, there can be a great diversity in family life.

As individuals go through life they change (and sometimes mature) in their thinking and attitudes. Societies also change, governments change, and so do families. Children grow up and, in time, replace their parents as the chief wage earners and molders of family values. At times there is healthy and beneficial growth, but at other times family members grow apart, develop conflicting values, and sometimes find themselves involved in family feuds. Then there are families which become "ingrown" and rigid. The husband and wife become so involved with one another and their children, that family members lose their individual identities and forget that God has called us not only to live together in harmony, but to serve and minister to others outside the home.

This brings us to a third conclusion. *To bring greatest growth and stability, families need other families for mutual encouragement and support.* Less than a hundred years ago—and in many parts of the world today—the dominant family pattern was the extended family: parents, children, grandparents, aunts, uncles, cousins, and close neighbors all living within the same community. Undoubtedly this was the style of family life experienced by people in Bible times. A whole group of relatives and neighbors helped each other, gave support in times of need, met together for fellowship or family celebrations, and experienced both mutual encouragement and family loyalty.

Our modern mobile age has dissolved such closeness. Family members are scattered and periodic "reunions" often become gatherings of related strangers. Even if we could return to the old ways of relating in the large extended family, most of us might not want it. We enjoy our freedom and are willing to sacrifice family togetherness in exchange for mobility.

It could be argued, however, that families still need other families. If our blood relatives are far away, isn't there value in finding substitute families with whom we can share, learn, and grow? These substitute family groups have been called "family clusters." Ideally they should include a group of families with diverse backgrounds, economic bases and styles of life. Single people, single-parent families, and people of diverse age groups should be included.[19] As a group these families can worship and relax together, give support and advice, and learn from one another. For many modern children, the only grandparents or aunts and uncles that they know are those who form part of a family cluster.

It isn't easy to form such a cluster although church family clusters sometimes come together spontaneously. As a start, it can be helpful to launch an adult Bible study which meets regularly and periodically includes gatherings with "all the kids."

In developing clusters, we must not forget the needs of our own families. If families are to be healthy and maturing, *we must commit ourselves to personal involvement with our own families.*

Recently, I talked with a Christian leader who expressed concern about tensions in his home and marriage. "I think I've reached a wrong conclusion," he stated. "I always thought that if I took care of my ministry, then God would take care of my family."

Such an idea has no basis in Scripture. Christians must recognize that one's calling as a parent or mate is every bit as important as a calling to the ministry or to some other vocation.

I often think of a statement made several years ago by the director of a large evangelical mission: "This mission can always get a new director; my kids can't get a new dad!" The man who said this travels all over the country preaching about the family, but the example of commitment to his own family surely carries at least as much weight as his seminars and sermons.

Reading books or articles, attending seminars, listening to sermons—all of these can help build family togetherness, but the place to start changing families must be in our own homes. Such personal involvement in our own families involves a commitment before God:

—to spend blocks of time with our families (beginning now—not at some vague time in the future);

—to constantly work at building and maintaining good communication in the home;

—to try always to understand and love our family members;

—to recognize that families involve grandparents and more distant relatives as well as our mates and children;

—to pray regularly *with* our family members and *for* their needs;

—to ask God to forgive and help us change when our work, hobbies, selfish interests, driving for success, church ministries, or other activities hinder and pull us away from our God-given responsibilities in the home; and

—to seek ways by which families can reach out to other families, including those in need, the aged, singles, students, and others who are away from relatives.

An old philosopher once stated that the journey of a thousand miles begins with the first step. Some believers have a long way to go in building better families; all of us could take at least some steps to improvements in family life.

It must be recognized that we all make mistakes in this area, and for some, such irreparable damage has been done that family togetherness will never be a reality. This realization can plunge people into quiet despair, but we must realize that our heavenly Father forgives totally, if we confess our sins (1 John 1:9). He will help us to go on from here, in spite of previous failures as family members.

Most people still have relatives, however, and for many there still is time to build better husband-wife, and parent-child relationships. Commitment to the family and to the permanence of marriage is a requirement for Christians, not an option. What good is life if we "gain the whole world" but lose our own families?

O come, let us sing for joy to the
Lord. . . . Come, let us worship and
bow down; Let us kneel before the
Lord our Maker. For He is our
God. . . . Enter His gates with thanks-
giving, And His courts with praise.
Give thanks to Him; bless His name.
For the Lord is good. . . .

Psalm 95:1, 6, 7; 100:4, 5

10
Meaningful Worship

During the 1960s, when the whole Western world seemed to be
swept along by waves of change, uncertainty, and dissatisfaction,
many Christians became excited about something called "church
renewal." Sermons were preached about it; students talked about it;
articles and books were written about it—and the basic message was
always the same: the church has become irrelevant and local con-
gregations are no longer meeting people's needs! The church, we
were told, must be renewed, updated, and made relevant.

It wasn't hard to spot the problems in many worship services. The
music was old-fashioned and often of poor quality—in contrast to
the seemingly flawless productions on television. Unlike the first
believers who spent their time in teaching, fellowship, the breaking
of bread and prayer (Acts 2:42) modern churches had become places
where the teaching was weak and unchallenging; the fellowship was
often strained and as artificial as a secular cocktail party; the breaking of bread seemed to be a cold ritual; and the prayer was cliché-
filled and neither spontaneous nor very relevant. In contrast to the
early church, many contemporary Christians had no sense of awe,
no conviction that God really works in our midst today, and little
concern for the needy. The Christian church which began with

gladness, sincerity and praise in the hearts of believers, had become dull, boring, and meaningless—especially to educated people.

This, of course, did not describe all churches, any more than it accurately pictures all bodies of believers today. Nevertheless, while some churches were alive, dynamic and growing, others were dying or already dead. Even people in the good churches realized that things could get better. While some tended to blame rigid Christian leaders for the problems and lack of progress in church, others might have agreed with the university president who once spoke to a student audience and suggested another cause of church deadness and meaningless worship.

> The chief reason why we get nothing out of (worship) is that we bring nothing with us except our own restricted natural egos. Thinking only of ourselves, we find only ourselves. And what we find is often drab and uninspiring. I suspect that anyone who does not really want to experience and commune with God will never do so; and I suspect that anyone who wants to do so will not fail.[1]

A. W. Tozer once noted that worship is "the missing jewel of the evangelical church." When we don't know how to worship in a way that is pleasing to God, our spiritual lives are certain to be dull, sometimes characterized by criticism and often longing for some kind of personal and church renewal.

But worship need not be unfulfilling and self-centered. Instead, it can be awe-inspiring and much more meaningful.

Meaningful Worship Is Both Propositional and Relational

Helping churches to become more relevant, to get back on target and to be more biblical has continued to concern many people since the church renewal movement began. Books, articles, seminars, and research projects have presented formulae for strengthening the churches and making them more like the worshiping, witnessing, teaching, caring bodies of believers that Christ intended.

In the midst of all this church renewal activity, however, a disturbing trend has developed—a tendency to line up something called "propositional theology" in contrast to "relational theology."[2]

Propositional theology (which is also known as transactional theology) emphasizes God's great transactions to human beings: the

Incarnation, the Substitutionary Atonement, Justification and Sanctification, for example. This is a theology which focuses attention on the foundation doctrines of Christianity; doctrines such as Christology (the person and work of Christ), ecclesiology (the doctrine of the church), and eschatology (the scriptural teachings about the future). Bible study becomes the core around which propositional theology develops and Christians are expected to respond with faith, love, obedience, and gratitude.

Relational (interpersonal) theology puts emphasis on the power of God to change persons and improve interpersonal relationships. According to Keith Miller, relational theology means "taking the basic Christian doctrines as foundational truths, making a commitment as total as possible of one's life, future and destiny with the people around you, with God and with yourself."[3]

Propositional theology tends to assume that if people believe the right things, they automatically become better persons with smooth interpersonal relationships. But what about the church members with a solid theology and good knowledge of the Bible who struggle with depression, cheat on their taxes, are cantankerous and spiteful in business meetings, and can't get along with their mates? For some reason their theology doesn't seem to be working. The problem, says the relational theologian, is that the more traditional propositional theology has been allowed to become so rigid, aloof and impersonal that the Bible no longer is presented as a book which touches lives. Relational theology is not then put forth as a humanistic alternative to the Bible. "Those of us who are identified with relational theology," writes Bruce Larson, "feel that it is an attempt to return to biblical theology, and to remind people of the two greatest commandments: love God and love our neighbor."[4]

Regretfully, some Christians have dug in their heels to uphold the foundation truths of Christianity but have refused to listen to the relationalists who maintain that the Bible can and must help us with our inner hurts and interpersonal conflicts. In contrast, there are others so concerned with building relationships and sharing in small group encounters that they have forgotten the biblical basis on which their Christianity must be built.

Obviously, we need a Christianity based solidly on the truths of God's Word *and* clearly applicable to the hurts and interpersonal conflicts that people struggle with today. We need a relational theology which stems from and is built on the propositional truths found in the Bible. We need pastors and church members who appreciate and can profit from relational theology without sacrificing or ignoring the value and foundation of propostional theology.

Deadness, irrelevancy, and lack of caring in the church arise when we depart from New Testament teachings, slip into a dull orthodoxy which has no practical relevance, or embrace the conclusions of a theology which has lost sight of its original biblical moorings. If our spiritual lives are to grow beyond a comfortable easy believism, we must learn how to worship God in a way which praises him and changes us. We need both the propositional and the relational emphasis.

Meaningful Worship Is Both Divine and Human

Worship could be defined as a human response to God's initiative. The worshiper centers his or her thoughts on God who, in turn, speaks to us personally in terms of our individual needs.

It is important to ponder the fact that worship is God's idea. When he was talking to the woman at the well, Jesus stated that the Father "seeks" people to worship him (John 4:23). Real worship is not something we do in response to social pressure, or because we are aroused by some ritual. Real worship is only possible because God has reached out to us, revealed himself to us, and sent the Holy Spirit who teaches us. "It's not *where* we worship that counts, but *how* we worship—is our worship spiritual and real? Do we have the Holy Spirit's help? For God is Spirit, and we must have his help to worship as we should. The Father wants this kind of worship from us" (John 4:22–23, LB). Indeed, he commands us to worship the Lord and to serve only him (Deut. 6:13; Matt. 4:10).

In the Old Testament, we read of a time when Moses went to talk with God, shortly after the people of Israel had been delivered from Egypt (Exod. 19). In that meeting, God declared that he wanted his people to be obedient and the answer which they gave surely pleased the Father: "All that the Lord has spoken we will do!"

It was at this point that God announced his intention to speak to the people. They had three days to prepare for the event by washing their clothes and consecrating themselves. They were warned not to get too close to the mountain where God would speak and at the appointed hour they trembled as the Lord revealed his presence by thunder, lightning, the appearance of a thick cloud and the sound of a very loud trumpet blast (Exod. 19:16).

As I re-read this scripture recently, I thought of the contrast between then and now. Because of Christ's death and resurrection, we can go directly to the Father with even our smallest petitions. Because we can read and have the written Word of God at our disposal, we can hear his Word whenever we wish. Perhaps because of God's goodness and nearness, however, we have lost our sense of awe and reverence. We have become so familiar with Christian theology and biblical teachings that we often take for granted those profound truths which God has revealed but which eluded thinking people for centuries.

The God whom we worship is the same God who revealed himself in the wilderness of Sinai. We know about his mercy, love, and compassion, but we easily forget about his sovereignty, power, and justice. Because we so often take God for granted, most of us have a tendency to approach worship too casually, and sometimes we get busy with Christian service and don't worship God at all.

Richard Foster has written about this clearly:

> If the Lord is to be the *Lord,* worship must have priority in our lives. The *first* commandment of Jesus is "Love the Lord your God with all your heart, and with all your soul, and with all your mind, and with all your strength" (Mark 12:30). The divine priority is worship first, service second. Our lives are to be punctuated with praise, thanksgiving and adoration. Service flows out of worship. Service as a substitute for worship is idolatry. Activity may become the enemy of adoration.[5]

Not long ago I visited a large church for the morning worship service and came away feeling like the hungry man who went seeking bread and was given a stone (Matt. 7:9). The building was beautiful, the choral anthem was magnificent and the people were very friendly. But the atmosphere was more like a Saturday night hoedown than an experience of worship. There was joking, applause, and constant whispering, but little emphasis on prayer and no mention of God's divine attributes. The pastor appeared to have a strong interest in himself and his "ministry" while ushers scurried about in busy activity throughout the whole service making concentration almost impossible.

I tried not to be critical but I left that service feeling cheated and frustrated. Few of us would want a return to those old time church services in which people never smiled, and even the most devout believers were engulfed in boredom. God surely was not honored by such deadness, but is he any more pleased with man-centered entertainment which masquerades as a "service of worship"? Have we allowed worship to "degenerate into entertainment built around the cult of personality"?[6] Have we forgotten that worship will never be genuine and pleasing to God until it loses its self-centered nature and seeks above all else to be a pure and holy adoration of Almighty God?[7]

A. W. Tozer has pinpointed this issue concisely in a comment which all of us would be wise to ponder seriously:

> The Church has surrendered her once lofty concept of God and has substituted for it one so low, so ignoble, as to be utterly unworthy of thinking, worshipping men. This she has not done deliberately, but little by little. . . .
>
> With our loss of the sense of majesty has come the further loss of religious awe and consciousness of the divine Presence. We have lost our spirit of worship and our ability to withdraw inwardly to meet God in adoring silence. . . . The words "Be still, and know that I am God" mean next to nothing to the self-confident, bustling worshiper in the middle period of the twentieth century. . . .
>
> The only way to recoup our spiritual losses is to go back to . . . a rediscovery of the majesty of God. . . . It is impossible to keep our moral practices sound and our inward attitudes right while our idea of God is erroneous or inadequate.[8]

When we think of worship as a human response to the nature and revelation of God we are kept from two major errors.[9] First there is the error of thinking that worship is solely to appease God and to "keep him happy." We must remember that there is "no element of superstition or magic in Christian worship. We are uninterested in manipulating God for our own ends, or in striking a bargain with the Almighty. This approach, called *do el deus* (give the god what he wants, and he will give you what you want) is one element that distinguished the idolatry of Rome and Greece from the worship of early Christians."[10]

Viewing worship as a response to the initiative of God also keeps us from the error of viewing worship as a technical production consisting of stirring oratory and polished performance. God wants worship from hearts which proclaim, "O come, let us worship and bow down, let us kneel before the Lord, our maker" (Ps. 95:6). Without such humble sincerity he is honored neither by a well-rehearsed and carefully planned liturgical service, nor an ill-prepared, shabby "meeting" at church.

It probably is true that few of us really know how to worship. It also seems true that really vibrant praise comes from believers who have a sure knowledge of who God is, a practical understanding of their position as sons and daughters of God and "teaching, reinforced by example, about what worship is and how to do it."[11]

The God who seeks our worship will surely show us how to worship in a way which honors him and changes us so that we become more Christlike. That is a basic reason for worship.

Meaningful Worship Is Both Objective and Subjective

In his Sermon on the Mount, Jesus gave a model prayer (Matt. 6:9–13) which can be divided into two parts. First there is the *objective* acknowledgment of God. We are to recognize his presence, honor his name, and submit to his sovereignty and will. Then, secondly, there is an emphasis on the *subjective*—that which applies to the worshiper. Only after giving praise to God do we focus on our needs, our guilt, and our struggles with temptation.

It has been suggested[12] that many Christian prayers, sermons and hymns can be divided into the objective and the subjective. Martin Luther's "A Mighty Fortress Is Our God" is an objective hymn which centers our attention on the majesty, sovereignty and power of God. In direct contrast "I Come to the Garden Alone" is so subjective that it uses the personal pronoun *I* twenty-seven times.

Which is better, the objective or subjective elements in worship? The answer, it seems, is "both." If worship really is "a human response to God's initiative," then it must focus both objectively on God and subjectively on the needs of the worshipers.

When the worshiper comes with an attitude of receptivity, expectancy and alertness, he or she can expect to be changed. If worship does not change us, it has not been worship. If it does not propel us into greater obedience it has not been effective.[13] As we reflect on a single service, we may not be able to see specific changes because the

. . . impact of worship is generally accumulative, not spasmodic or momentary. This is to say that worship cultivates the spiritual sensitivity in the individual so that he gradually but surely modifies his ways and makes those adjustments within himself and between himself, others, and God which mark his progress in Christlikeness. Through regularity and frequency of worship, one is changed bit by bit in the direction of those objectives which are concerned in the worshipping community. In like fashion, he is blessed by those curative powers which worship releases into the stream of his daily experiences.[14]

Consistent worship of God and meditation on his characteristics always go along with a consideration of our own needs and attributes. When worship is solely objective it tends to be cold and seemingly irrelevant. When worship is primarily subjective it is human-centered and powerless. Like the two theologies which we discussed earlier in this chapter: neither an objective nor a subjective emphasis in worship is complete without the other. We need both. I can't think of any person in the Bible who really met God in worship and came away unchanged.

Meaningful Worship Must Be Singular and Corporate

As we have discussed worship in this chapter the emphasis has been on "corporate worship"—the experience of meeting together with other believers so that God can be praised and exalted by the Christian community. Of course worship is also possible when we come to God alone and worship in solitude. To be complete we need worship which is both singular and corporate.

Singular Worship

In the midst of a changing, demanding society, how can modern individuals find the time and motivation to consider God? This question is not easy to answer but three guidelines may be helpful.

First, we can *practice the presence of God.*

Brother Lawrence was a lowly and poorly educated Frenchman who lived three hundred years ago as a lay brother among the Carmelites in Paris. Little is known about his background except for a small collection of observations and letters which expressed his views of God and were published under the title *The Practice of the Presence of God.*

According to a recent publisher of this ancient classic, Brother Lawrence was:

No conceited scholar . . . theological and doctrinal debates bored him, if he noticed them at all. His one desire was for communion with God. We find him worshiping more in his kitchen than in his cathedral; he could pray, with another

> Love of all pots and pans and things . . .
> Make me a saint by getting meals
> And washing up the plates!

and he could say, "The time of business does not with me differ from the time of prayer, and in the noise and clatter of my kitchen, while several persons are at the same time calling for different things, I possess God in as great tranquility as if I were upon my knees at the blessed sacrament."[15]

Brother Lawrence believed that there was no distinction between a time of business and a time of worship. He determined to pray short prayers all day and to think about God continually. At first this was painful and very difficult, but over time and with deliberate "practice" Lawrence learned to be in constant communication with his Creator. Is it impossible for us to do the same? Surely we too can learn to keep in constant mental contact with the one who sticks closer than a brother (Prov. 18:24). Writing to a young priest, Bernard of Clairvaux stated this powerfully: "Now abideth speech, example, prayer, these three, but the greatest of these is prayer."

Second, we can *pray and meditate at specified times.*

Throughout our Christian lives most of us have heard spiritual leaders talk about the importance of "personal devotions"—private and regularly scheduled times set aside for communication with God. Jesus, who worshiped regularly in the temple (Luke 4:16), also encouraged the disciples to pray in private, and he himself spent time early in the morning (Mark 1:35) and in the evening (Mark 6:47) in prayer and solitary meditation. Paul, who worshiped with others and preached in corporate gatherings (Acts 20:7), also engaged in private prayer (Phil. 1:4; Col. 1:9; 1 Thess. 3:10) and wrote of the importance of Bible study (2 Tim. 3:15), fasting (2 Cor. 11:27) and the pursuit of godliness (1 Tim. 3). Clearly, the believer must find time for personal worship in addition to his or her participation in church services.

I am somewhat concerned about those people who never set aside the time for personal prayer but whose private worship is fit into the schedule only when there is opportunity. In this busy era of history there rarely is time for everything that we might intend to do. Something usually is left undone and one of the activities that most often gets pushed out is time alone with God. Perhaps Forsyth is correct in his suggestion that for Christians "the worst sin is

prayerlessness" since this indicates an indifference toward God.[16]
Prayerlessness is most apparent in those who never set aside specific
time to pray.

I once read a book written by a famous writer who was describing
her experiences as an author. "If I wait until I get inspired to write,
I'll never put anything on paper," she concluded. "I write every
day, whether I feel like it or not and the inspiration comes *after* I get
started."

Private worship is like that. We don't always feel like praying or
reading Scripture. Sometimes to do this is a struggle[17] and most of
us would agree with Calvin that we will never pray unless we urge
and force ourselves.[18] Inspiration (and growth) come only when we
set time aside on a regular basis—preferably daily—to spend with
God whether we feel like it or not. If it means getting up early,
blocking off some time in our appointment book or turning off the
TV at a given hour—it is important to set aside time for God, just
like we set time aside to eat and sleep.

And how should this time be spent? Nobody can answer that
question for another and there is danger in giving guidelines which
could be turned into a rigid formulae. Nevertheless, it may help to
be reminded that many people begin by asking God to guide their
thoughts and to teach them how to worship. Some like to read a
psalm or two because these focus so completely on God's attributes,
and then they read a selection from both the Old and New Testament. It can help to take notes on what you are learning and there is
value in frequently looking at a Bible commentary or devotional
literature.

Then you may want to pray in accordance with the ACTS acro-
nym which has been mentioned in so many sermons.

A—adoration of God
C—confession of sin to God
T—thanksgiving to God
S—supplication—bringing of requests to God

It has been suggested that few Christians spend more than ten
minutes a day in prayer and meditation on the Scriptures. While it is
true that length of time with God probably is less important than
quality of time, it surely shows what we think of prayer and meditation if this becomes an appendix to life, squeezed into our schedules

when and if we can find the time. Think what a marriage would be like if the husband or wife gave the same quantity and quality of time to a spouse that we are inclined to give to God!

In Mark 9 we read about a boy who was brought to the disciples for healing, but who didn't get any help. Apparently, in their haste to be of service, the disciples had forgotten an important lesson— the crucial place of prayer (Mark 9:29).

Perhaps these disciples were like us—so busy with the demands of living, and sometimes with serving, that they had no time to pray. So often prayer is *thought to be* important—we all agree to that—but prayer is then pushed to the periphery of life and we try to move ahead in our own strength and self-sufficiency. Is it surprising that our spiritual lives often seem so weak and our efforts ineffective?

Those dedicated men and women who have written books about prayer and meditation seem to agree that our regular periods of solitude must be supplemented, periodically, by extra times for communication with God. An evening or half-day of prayer, a weekend alone, a time of prayer with one's family or a trusted friend—these can all pay rich dividends in terms of added spiritual vigor. Surely Henri Nouwen is correct in his conclusion that when "solitude is not an integral part of early life we quickly start becoming deaf to God's demands and become mostly concerned with doing 'my thing.'"[19]

It may also be that private meditation must become a more regular part of our lives before we are ready for the third guideline for singular worship.

We can *prepare for corporate worship.*

Sometimes I think the devil is most active on Sunday morning. How often before leaving for church, do we oversleep, discover that some article of clothing isn't pressed, yell at the kids because they are dawdling, and say unkind things to each other as everyone scrambles to be ready on time? When we get to church we can't find a parking place and then disturb everyone as we squeeze into a back pew because we don't want to "march down to the front when we are late." Instead of arriving with a spirit of expectancy, we come to church feeling rushed, tired, frustrated and often irritable. This doesn't happen to everyone and it doesn't happen all the time, but too often we do arrive too flustered to worship and we go home wondering why we "didn't get anything out of the service."

A better approach is to arrive early—even if that means getting up and leaving home earlier. As other worshipers arrive, pray for the church leaders and the other people in the congregation. Ask God to keep your mind from wandering, to speak to you during the service, to give you an attitude of worship, and to keep you free of criticism. (The service will mean little to you if your mind is focused on criticizing the actions of those who are worshiping with you.)

When the service begins, think about the words of the hymns, pray along with the pastor (how often does your mind wander during the pastoral prayer?) and take notes on the sermon.

All of this, I am convinced, takes practice and is likely to be interspersed with failure. God is patient, however, and if we can be patient with ourselves we will begin to see improvement.

Corporate Worship

Sociologists and psychologists have been quick to point out that there are great individual differences in our preferences for worship. In choosing a place to worship each Christian is influenced by his or her upbringing, past experiences, personality, education, socio-economic level, and sometimes by one's racial or ethnic background.

The New Testament does not tell us specifically how, where or when to worship except to state that Christ, God's Son, is to be central, the Holy Spirit is to be our guide, and all things are to be done in an orderly manner (1 Cor. 14:40).

Seven practices appear to have characterized worship in the early church: prayer, praise (including thanksgiving and the singing of hymns), confession of sin, reaffirmation of one's faith (including baptism), reading the Scriptures, preaching (including teaching), and participation in the Lord's Supper communion service. In all of this there was fellowship with other believers and probably the taking of at least periodic collections.[20] Even in Bible times these gatherings differed in accordance with local circumstances, which included the political state in which the worshipers lived. In the Scriptures we read of larger meetings (see Acts 2, for example), but at times these were forbidden and the Christians had to meet quietly in houses or secretly in small catacombs underground. Regardless of the circumstances we can learn from the sixth chapter of Isaiah what worship can be like. The king, Uzziah, had died and when Isaiah worshiped in the temple he had a deep and moving encounter with God. Isaiah apparently went to worship with an attitude of expectancy, and he was not disappointed.

God spoke and Isaiah heard (Isa. 6:1, 8).
There was praise and Isaiah participated (vv. 2–4).
Isaiah confessed his sin (v. 6) and God forgave (v. 8).
God called for commitment and Isaiah responded (v. 8).
God sent Isaiah to serve, and the prophet obeyed (vv. 9f).

This brief example brings us to a final but significant observation about meaningful worship.

Meaningful Worship Is Active, Not Passive

If world history continues for another century or two, future historians are likely to point to the invention of television as one of the most revolutionary events of our age. Suddenly people were yanked from isolationism and narrow parochialism, and pulled into the fast-moving world of the twentieth century. While there are some people who ignore television or choose to not even own a TV set, many more have become captives of the tube. Passively we watch news events even while they are happening and we listen to the history-molding statements of world leaders. We can watch plays, travelogues, sports events, historical ceremonies, and musicians in living color, and we are able to get closer to these events through television than would ever be possible otherwise. Our values are shaped by television writers and our buying habits are molded by carefully produced advertisements.

It is not surprising, therefore, that we take this television mentality to church. The television viewer is expected to be passive and we often arrive for worship with the same mindset. We have come as an audience to be entertained by the music and inspired by the speaker. The sanctuary is an "auditorium" where "spectators" come to observe, audit, and often to critique the performance. If the service gets a good review we return the following week; if not, we determine to catch a different show someplace else on subsequent Sundays.

Such a portrayal is not meant to be cynical. I have purposely overdrawn the picture in an attempt to illustrate an attitude which, regretfully, many people take to church, and which is a tendency that can tempt all of us.

But to paraphrase President John F. Kennedy, believers must ask not "what can my church do for me" but "what can I do for my church?" One answer is that we can approach worship with anticipation and be actively involved in prayer, scriptural meditation, and other forms of involvement.

It is true that salvation comes as a gift to anyone who is a believer in Christ (Eph. 2:8, 9; John 3:16). It is not true that the Christian then is free to sit back passively and do nothing except to bask in an easy-believism religion. The Scriptures are filled with instructions and admonitions to get involved actively. God, who once expected his people to offer sacrifices of bulls and goats, now expects us to offer ourselves, actively praising God with our lips and following this with sharing and acts of doing good (Rom. 12:1, 2; Heb. 13:15, 16).

To some people, Mother Teresa must have seemed an unlikely candidate for the Nobel Peace Prize. Unlike so many of the statesmen and world leaders who had previously received this honor, Mother Teresa had led no mass movements and neither had she negotiated any peace treaties. A humble woman who shuns publicity and doesn't like biographies because they glorify people, this remarkable woman has given her life to serving God and serving the destitute, dying people of Calcutta.

When Malcolm Muggeridge went to India to film a documentary on Mother Teresa's work, he was deeply impressed. "I never met anyone less sentimental . . . more down to earth," he wrote later. "Every day Mother Teresa meets Jesus; first at the Mass whence she derives sustenance and strength; then in each needing, suffering soul she sees and tends. . . . Thus for Mother Teresa the two commandments—to love God and to love our neighbor—are jointly fulfilled; indeed inseparable."[21]

Probably in this world there are many more people like Mother Teresa—people who serve in anonymity. Nevertheless, I wonder if God is saddened to observe that a person like this nun is so rare that she receives a Nobel Prize. Shouldn't we all be like her, wherever we live? Her goal is to obey Christ and to be like Jesus. Her life reflects regular corporate and private worship which blossoms forth into godly living and dedicated service.

Most of us need to learn how to worship like that. It is a crucial pathway in the road to spiritual maturity.

Thou art my hope; O Lord God, Thou
art my confidence. . . .

Psalm 71:5

How blessed is he whose . . . hope is
in the Lord his God.

Psalm 146:5

This hope we have as an anchor of the
soul, a hope both sure and
steadfast. . . .

Hebrews 6:19

11

Realistic Hope

The apostle Paul knew what it is like to face opposition. Not only
was he beaten, jailed, and ridiculed (2 Cor. 11:24–28); he constantly faced opponents who resisted his authority and disagreed
with his teachings.

In the town of Corinth, for example, some people challenged the
central Christian view that human beings will rise from the dead.
These critics had concluded that "dead men stay dead—forever"—
a viewpoint which the apostle attacked vigorously and decisively
(1 Cor. 15:12–19). If there is no resurrection, Paul stated, then
Christ is still dead, our faith is useless, we are deluded, humans are
still bogged down in sin and there is no hope for the future. If this
life is all the existence that we have, then we are to be pitied—the
victims and peddlers of an empty religion.

I thought about this recently during a meeting overseas with some
youth leaders. "Teenagers in our country have no hope," my
Christian hosts reported. "Our young people expect that nuclear
war or economic collapse will come sooner or later. They see no
need to get an education or to prepare for the future. They have no
religion, no clear values, and no drive. They are modern examples
of an old philosophy which Jesus condemned—the view that we

should take it easy, eat, drink, and be merry since we probably will die tomorrow."

Such thinking is not limited to frustrated students in other countries. It has permeated our own society. It gives rise to a "what's the use" attitude which philosophers call "existential despair," psychologists term "meaninglessness," and all of us recognize as "hopelessness."

The End of Easy Believism

In an article written several years ago, one of my professors observed that most modern people believe deeply in the importance of being happy. Since unhappiness is seen as a sign of maladjustment, many lives are consumed with a search for happiness.[1]

During the second world war an Austrian psychiatrist named Viktor Frankl was imprisoned by the Nazis in Europe. Amidst the horrors of that concentration camp, none of the prisoners was happy but this apparently had little to do with their mental health. Some of the prisoners—those who saw no reason for living—buckled under the tension and soon died. In contrast, the prisoners who survived were those who believed that there could be purpose in life, even for them. "I venture to say," Frankl wrote later, that "there is nothing in the world . . . that would so effectively help one to survive even the worst conditions, as the knowledge that there is meaning in one's life."[2] Frankl and the other survivors never lost hope.

Is it too strong to conclude that countless people in our society have lost both the ability to be happy and the stability which comes from having meaning and hope in their lives? We are surrounded by those who try to find happiness and meaning through self-indulgence, novelty, and the pursuit of "personal peace and affluence." Like the early Christians at Laodicea, these people proclaim that they are rich, healthy, clear-minded and needing nothing when in reality all of us are wretched, miserable, poor, blind and naked (Rev. 3:17). Like the Laodiceans we still believe in God, but for many, religion has become a lukewarm easy believism which is largely impotent, and not very fulfilling. In churches the people sing about peace and joy, but inwardly many who call themselves Christians have little happiness, hardly any meaning in life, and no real hope.

Malcolm Muggeridge has described this condition with great
clarity. Nuclear warfare may destroy us some day, he wrote, but it
is more likely that our civilization will crumble because of . . .

the degeneracy of a population grown soft by excessive self-indulgence
and confused by the collapse of standards of belief and behavior which
have hitherto been acceptable to them. . . . Previous civilizations have
been overthrown from without by the incursion of barbarian hordes.
Christendom has dreamed up its own dissolution in the minds of its own
intellectual elite. Our barbarians are home products, indoctrinated at the
public expense, urged on by the media systematically stage by stage,
dismantling Christendom, depreciating and deprecating all its values.
The whole social structure is now tumbling down, dethroning its God,
undermining all its certainties. All this, wonderfully enough, is being
done in the name of the health, wealth, and happiness of all man-
kind. . . . I could go on giving details, but you can very well fill in for
yourselves: the internecine conflicts between the Western nations, the
decline of Western power and influence, the . . . cultural decline of
Western art and literature. . . . Another area of the moral and spiritual
decline of Christendom is the abandonment of Christian mores. The
movement away from Christian moral standards has not meant moving
to an alternative humanistic system of moral standards as was antici-
pated, but moving into a moral vacuum, especially in the areas of
eroticism. . . . The West is also on a quest for security and plenty. The
quest for security has given us a weapon so powerful that it can blow us
and our earth to smithereens; our quest for plenty has resulted in the
exploitation of our resources to an unconscionable degree . . . as the
American social critic Leslie Fiedler put it, "We continue to insist that
change is progress, self-indulgence is freedom and novelty is original-
ity."[3]

In contrast to the thinking of this world in which we live, Christians must have a different perspective.

As Christians we know that here we have no continuing city, that
crowns roll in the dust and every earthly kingdom must sometime
flounder, whereas we acknowledge a king men did not crown and cannot dethrone, as we are citizens of a city of God they did not build and
cannot destroy. Thus the apostle Paul wrote to the Christians in Rome,
living in a society as depraved and dissolute as ours. Their games, like
our television, specialized in spectacles of violence and eroticism. Paul
exhorted them to be steadfast, unmovable, always abounding in God's
work, to concern themselves with the things that are unseen, for the
things which are seen are temporal but the things which are not seen are
eternal.[4]

Instead of moaning about the moral decline around us, Muggeridge concludes that the present state of our society can give us a

reason for rejoicing. When people begin to see "the decay of institutions and instruments of power, see intimations of empires falling to pieces, money in total disarray . . . (and) when every earthly hope has been explored and found wanting," it is then that "Christ's hand reaches out sure and firm."[5] Like the alcoholic who "hits bottom" before he or she can admit the problem and accept help, so modern human beings are being forced to see the futility, meaninglessness and hopelessness of a life without God.

The Basis of Hope

Within recent years a number of political, media, and spiritual leaders have commented on the state of our society. Some are pessimistic about the declining moral and economic status of our nation, but others express optimism and hope.

In a sense, such hope is good. It keeps us going—just like hope keeps terminally ill patients alive, even while they struggle with denial, anger, depression and declining health.[6]

Hope could be defined as the desire for some thing or some goal which we want but which is not completely within our power to attain. The student hopes to pass an examination. The patient hopes to recover. The airline passenger hopes that the plane will not crash. Each of these experiences involves an element of uncertainty often mixed with anxiety, fearfulness and some expectation of what might happen.

Hope can be strong or weak depending on three issues: how important it is to get what we want, how likely it is that our desires will be fulfilled, and whether other people around us also have hope. When a doctor or the family loses hope for a patient's recovery, the sick person often loses hope as well and death comes quickly.[7] In contrast, when hope persists in others there is more likely to be recovery and much less despair in the patient.

All of this has great relevance for our spiritual lives and our psychological stability. When people lose hope in their country, in their fellow human beings and in themselves, they begin to "fall apart" psychologically and sometimes spiritually. They lose their enthusiasm, plunge into discouragement or hedonistic self-indulgence, and stop trying to improve themselves or their society. They become like the people of Jeremiah's day who complained: "It's hopeless! For we are going to follow our own plans, and each of us will act according to the stubbornness of his evil heart'' (Jer. 18:12).

The sincere follower of Jesus Christ never has to conclude that all is hopeless. Like everyone else, believers hope to keep healthy, pass exams, avoid accidents, and attain success, but our ultimate hope is in something much more stable than the vicissitudes of life. Our hope is in the all-powerful God who is unchanging and who has kept his promises to human beings without fail and for centuries. When everything else in life disintegrates, we can stand firm like Job and like David who knew that their only secure hope was in God (Job 13:15; Ps. 39:7).

I am told that it was William Hulme who once said, ''Because I know the Who, I can endure the what, even without knowing the why.'' That could be a concise expression of Christian hope. Our hope is in God who exists eternally, loves unconditionally, never changes, and always keeps his promises—even though our minds often cannot fully comprehend his ways.

Clearly for the Christian there is a close connection between hope and faith (1 Peter 1:21). According to the Book of Hebrews (11:1) ''faith is the assurance of things hoped for, the conviction of things not seen.'' Because we have faith in God and in his sovereignty, our hopes are more than wishful thinking. We know that God's promises *will* be fulfilled so we can put ourselves at his disposal and relax on a hope that is ''both sure and steadfast'' (Heb. 6:19). Without God, there isn't much reason for hope (Eph. 2:12), but when we come to God, we can sing with David who wrote,

> Lord, for what do I wait?
> My hope is in Thee. . . .
> I waited patiently for the Lord;
> And He inclined to me, and heard my cry.
> He brought me up out of the pit of
> destruction, out of the miry clay; And
> He set my feet upon a rock making my
> footsteps firm.
> And He put a new song in my mouth,
> a song of praise to our God; Many will
> see and fear, And will trust in the Lord . . .
> Why are you in despair, O my soul?
> And why have you become disturbed within
> me?
> Hope in God (Pss. 39:7; 40:1–3; 42:5).

There are several reasons which lead believers to lose sight of this biblical hope. First, and perhaps most devastating, we lose hope when we accept the standards of a society which tries to find happiness, meaning and security in things instead of in God.

The terror which reigned in Uganda during the days of Idi Amin will never be understood by those of us who lived elsewhere and heard only passing news reports of the intense suffering which so many Ugandan people experienced. Amin wanted to eliminate Christianity from Uganda, but instead the church grew under persecution.[8] The people gave away their possessions freely because they realized that security is not found in money, status, insurance, military might, government stability, or the abundance of possessions (Luke 12:15). Our hope and security are in God alone. Most of us give lip service to this conclusion but sometimes this doesn't much affect our life styles or values.

Second, we lose hope when we separate hope from faith and love. First Corinthians 13 is such a powerful sermon on love that we forget how Paul linked hope with faith and love (1 Cor. 13; Col. 1:4, 5). Can we really hope in God if our faith is shaky or our lives are not very loving?

Faith, hope and love do not appear spontaneously in human beings. Usually these traits come to people who sincerely want them and it is probable that the three characteristics arise most often in children whose parents consistently model faith, hope and love. These are divinely given attributes (Luke 17:5; 1 Thess. 3:12; Rom. 5:1–5; 15:4, 5) and individuals who want real hope, accompanied by faith and love, must ask God to bestow these upon us.

Third, we lose hope when we forget that each of us is here to fit into God's program for the world.[9] Nonbelievers may want to accept this, but most find it inconceivable that God "loves us and has a wonderful plan" for each life. It is a plan which includes specialized service, the giving of unique gifts (Rom. 12), and often the presence of sufferings like those which came into the life of Job, dominated the life of Jesus, and have influenced millions of believers throughout world history.

This suggests a fourth reason why we lose hope. Too often we convince ourselves, and each other, that if we "have enough faith and hope," all problems will disappear. When the problems persist we begin to doubt God's power or willingness to hear our prayers. With the coming of this doubt, hope begins to fade.

Recently I wrote an article on homosexuality and suggested that for some people the struggle with homosexual tendencies may persist for a lifetime. The magazine editor quietly removed my sentence and substituted a statement which implied that inner turmoil would always disappear from the lives of those who hope in Christ. But the Bible does not teach this. Some believers struggle with depression, doubt, confusion or homosexuality for their entire lives. Some develop illnesses and physical handicaps which never go away. Like Paul, some Christians are given a "thorn in the flesh," which is not taken away in spite of frequent prayers for deliverance (2 Cor. 12:7–9).

Instead of losing his hope and joy because of these weaknesses, Paul recognized that afflictions could both strengthen his faith and increase his effectiveness as a servant of Jesus Christ. The apostle might have agreed with an old fable which has been told about a grandfather clock.

For three generations, the clock had stood in the same corner, faithfully ticking off the minutes and hours. Each day, the clock's owner grasped the chain and pulled up the heavy weight to keep the clock running.

Then a new owner appeared and concluded that the clock should not have to bear so heavy a load. Gently, he removed the weight and immediately the old clock stopped ticking.

"Why did you remove my weight?" the clock asked.

"I wanted to lighten your load," replied the man.

"That doesn't help," the clock responded. "Please put the weight back on the chain. That weight is what keeps me going."

The moral of this little fable is obvious. A life without burdens isn't necessarily a triumphant life. Often burdens "keep us going" and help us mature. That is cause for thanksgiving and hope.

How, then, is hope instilled in ourselves and in others—even when we don't feel hopeful? We have already noted that we can ask God to give hope. Then we can search the Scriptures to find and meditate on those passages which give reassurance and certainty in these times of instability. We also can try to rid our minds of self-defeating ideas. which say "there is no hope—give up!" (Often such conclusions are not even based on solid facts.) Then we can get involved in helping others. Loving actions can cause despair to disintegrate and can arouse hope—especially if we see that our actions are accomplishing something worthwhile.[10]

The Mask of Spirituality

I never cease to be amazed at the honesty with which the Bible describes the spiritual giants of the faith. Noah, Abraham, Jacob, David, Peter and a host of others were mighty men of faith whose failures and sins are recorded in Scripture along with reports of their great spiritual victories.

Moses was such a man. Chosen by God to do a great work, Moses rose to the challenge, faithfully led the Israelites out of Egypt and brought God's people to the edge of the Promised Land. But Moses had weaknesses including one that was not recorded in Scripture until New Testament times.

After he came down from Mount Sinai with the Ten Commandments, Moses' face shone so brightly that his friends were afraid to come near. It is worth noting that Moses didn't know about this at first but his whole countenance was brightened because he had been with the Lord (Exod. 34:29, 30). Apparently this shining face appeared repeatedly—whenever God met with his servant—so it was decided that a veil would be worn to cover the face of Moses and to shield the brightness while he moved among the people.

But Moses grew accustomed to wearing the veil and instead of using it to diffuse the brightness of his shining face, he wore the veil to hide the fact that the glory was fading. The children of Israel must have gone on believing that Moses was a spiritual giant with a radiant testimony but in reality he apparently was growing spiritually dull (2 Cor. 3:7–18).

Is it possible that many modern believers are like Moses? In times past we have had close encounters with God—encounters which left us radiant and filled with a deep sense of awe and inner peace. Even now we wear the veil of evangelical respectability and Christian orthodoxy, but inside there is little real commitment to the Lord and only a mild willingness to embrace Christ-honoring values. We find "good" reasons to justify our life styles and the pursuit of affluence while we hide behind a mask of pious clichés and respectable easy believism. We become church members like those described several years ago by Keith Miller—"people who outwardly look contented and at peace but inwardly are crying out for someone to love them . . . just as they are—confused, frustrated, often frightened, guilty, and often unable to communicate even within their own families." Is it still true that the "modern church is filled with many people who look pure, sound pure, and are inwardly sick of themselves, their weaknesses, their frustration, and the lack of reality around them in the church?''[11]

If this picture is accurate, can we change? How shall we live filled with real hope and without the sickly religion of easy believism? In his second letter to the Corinthians, Paul gives a formula which can provide the answer.

1. *We must forsake religious phoniness and recognize that our strength comes from God alone.* In our own strength none of us can live lives which honor God. We either pretend that we are spiritually alert, or conclude that we must stop pretending and admit that ''our adequacy is from God'' (2 Cor. 3:5). Paul did not lose heart in the midst of his Christian work because he remembered the ministry that God had given him, remembered God's great mercy, and took care to reject the ''craftiness'' or phoniness which could have crept into his own life (2 Cor. 4:1, 2).

Perhaps the apostle would have applauded Harriet Beecher Stowe whose book, *Uncle Tom's Cabin,* sold 300,000 copies in the first year. It was translated into numerous languages and described by a British statesman as the volume which had done more for humanity than any other book of fiction. Tolstoy ranked it among the great achievements of the human mind and others agreed that more than anything else it served to advance the cause of freedom from slavery.

But Harriet Beecher Stowe refused to take credit for what she had written. ''I, the author of *Uncle Tom's Cabin?''* she exclaimed. ''No, indeed, I could not control the story; it wrote itself. The Lord wrote it, and I was but the humblest instrument in His hand. It came to me in visions, one after another, and I put them down in words. To Him alone be the praise!''

Like innumerable Christians who have lived before her and after, this lady discovered that her ''adequacy was of God.'' Aware of her own inadequacy, she yielded herself as an instrument in the Master's hand.[12] This surely was at the basis of her own spiritual stability and hope in the midst of trying times.

2. *We must submit to the transforming power of the Holy Spirit.* The modern Charismatic movement has been criticized at times for some of its excesses, including easy-believism tendencies of its own. Nevertheless, this movement has pointed afresh to the power of the Holy Spirit, and has demonstrated how this same Spirit trans-

forms lives. "Where the Spirit of the Lord is, there is liberty," Paul writes (2 Cor. 3:17). There is also spiritual growth and depth.

Easy believism distracts us from depending on the Holy Spirit. It is a way of thinking and acting which must grieve and quench the Spirit even as it lulls us into spiritual atrophy. Whenever we turn to the Lord in humility and renewed dedication, the phoniness, apathy, and other veils are taken away (2 Cor. 3:16). God sees us in all of our imperfections but then his Holy Spirit begins to transform us into what he wants us to be (2 Cor. 3:18).

3. *We must seek to bring glory to God in all that we do.* When Viktor Frankl wrote about our "search for meaning," he concluded that each person must find his or her own unique purpose in life.

In one sense Frankl was right. Each of us has unique gifts and responsibilities and we must seek to find God's special place of service. In another respect, however, Frankl missed the clear biblical teaching that in all we do, our purpose in life must be to bring glory to God (1 Peter 4:11; 2 Cor. 4:15).

This is sometimes easier said than done, but the Bible does give some practical guidelines. We bring glory to God when we: keep our minds alert so that we can pray continually (1 Peter 4:7; 1 Thess. 5:17); show hospitality and love to others (1 Peter 4:8; John 13:12); and determine to serve Christ with the gifts and opportunities he has given (1 Peter 4:10, 11). Often we will fail—that is a part of being human—but with the Holy Spirit's help we can seek to obey his commandments in all that we do (John 13:10), even if our nonbelieving *and* believing friends try to lure us into a continuation of comfortable easy believism.

4. *We can accept the fact that life might not be easy.* As we have seen, the Bible never leaves us with the idea that believers will have easy, problem-free lives. Paul himself experienced numerous persecutions (2 Cor. 11:24–28) but he had learned to grow both in spite of and because of his afflictions. Listen to his confidence in the midst of difficulties:

> We are afflicted in every way, but not crushed; perplexed, but not despairing; persecuted but not forsaken; struck down, but not destroyed. . . .
> We do not lose heart, but though our outer man is decaying, yet our inner man is being renewed day by day. For momentary light affliction is producing for us an eternal weight of glory far beyond all comparison, while we look out at the things which are seen, but at the things which

are not seen; for the things which are seen are temporal, but the things which are not seen are eternal (2 Cor. 4:8, 9, 16–18).

5. *We must be people of gratitude.* Biologist Hans Selye wrote a book[13] in 1956 which initiated a flood of research and, more than anything else, stimulated popular and professional interest in the psychology of stress.

Selye's book was both technical and controversial, but some statements near the end of his volume may have been lost in the debate which centered on the famous doctor's other ideas. "It seems to me," he wrote, that . . .

> Among all the emotions, there is one which, more than any other, accounts for the absence or presence of stress in human relations; that is the feeling of gratitude—with its negative counterpart, the need for revenge. . . . I think in the final analysis that *gratitude and revenge are the most important factors governing our actions in everyday life;* upon them also chiefly depend our peace of mind, our feelings of security or insecurity, of fulfillment, or frustration, in short, the extent to which we can make a success of life.[14]

Selye goes on to discuss revenge in a way which reminds one of Hebrews 12:15. Like the biblical author, Selye concludes that all kinds of trouble stem from bitterness.

> Revenge . . . has no virtue whatever, and can only hurt both the giver and the receiver of its fruits. The seeds of any fruit can only reproduce the tree they come from. Revenge generates more revenge; gratitude tends to incite still more gratitude. No sane person would consciously select the savage satisfactions of the vendetta as an ultimate aim in life. But "Gratitude is the sign of Noble souls."[15]

Instead of revenge, criticism and bitterness, we must develop the habit of giving thanks. Rather than complaints and griping, we must let our minds dwell on those things which are honorable, right, pure, lovely, good, excellent, and worthy of praise (Phil. 4:8). This thankful kind of attitude pleases God and brings him glory (2 Cor. 4:15).

The Future of Believers

Not long ago our family decided that the time had come to purchase a new car. After visiting a number of showrooms we made our selection and began the process of arranging for delivery of our new vehicle. In the midst of this, our salesman was called away to be with his wife while she gave birth to their first child.

On the following day the man was euphoric.

"When I saw that baby being born," he exclaimed, "it seemed that everything else in the whole world was insignificant in comparison!"

A few days later I thought of this as one of my former students told of his serious brain surgery. Without any warning he had collapsed in a parking lot and was whisked to a hospital where a team of surgeons removed a grapefruit-size tumor. In commenting on this experience my friend was somber with gratitude.

"I'm alive!" he said.

"I can see! I can walk! I can talk! Some of the issues which concerned me before surgery—getting ahead and accumulating material things, for example—no longer seem important. I am tremendously thankful for the things which I once took for granted."

Tragedies, life crises, sickness, even the birth of a child, are events which sober us, and force us to give attention to the really important things in life. At such times we recognize that easy believism is a weak religion. It doesn't help much when we face the sobering and eternally important issues of life.

It is then that the social acceptability of religion is no longer important, the pat answers often fail to satisfy, and we have little interest in church-related entertainment or in the desire for self-centered success.

At such times, we discover that a truly biblical and truly helpful faith is one characterized by issues similar to those discussed in these pages: costly commitment, solid intellectualism, stable emotionalism, a separated life style, selfless success, a giving love, sanctified sex, a changed home life, meaningful worship, and a realistic hope.

As we grow older in the Christian life, most of us begin to recognize that God is very patient. He tolerates our unfaithfulness, repeatedly forgives our sins, and remains available to us even when we ignore him.

But God's patience does not last forever, and eventually most of us recognize that he doesn't give us many years to serve him on this earth. When we are teenagers, death seems far away and life seems like an eternity. The years roll by quickly, however, and all too soon we realize the truth in that little couplet which many of us heard as young believers: Only one life, it will soon be past; only what's done for Christ will last! The easy believism which has been challenged in these pages will someday be "weighed in the balances and found to be deficient." It will be revealed for what it is: a comfortable religion which distracts many believers from the fullness of true spirituality.

Near the end of his life, the apostle John was banished to the Isle of Patmos where he had the remarkable vision which is recorded in the Book of Revelation. On several occasions in that Revelation Jesus Christ warns that he will be returning someday—perhaps soon.

When he comes what will he find in his church on earth?

What will he find in your church?

What will he find in your family?

What kind of a religion will he find in you?

Notes

Preface

1. From the Preface to A. W. Tozer's *Renewed Day by Day: A Daily Devotional* (compiled by G. B. Smith). (Grand Rapids: Baker, 1980).
2. Henri J. M. Nouwen. *The Genesee Diary: Report from a Trappist Monastery*. (Garden City, New York: Imagi Books, 1981), pp. 122, 123.
3. Richard J. Foster. *Freedom of Simplicity*. (San Francisco: Harper & Row, 1981), p. 26.

Chapter 1

1. Harold C. Warlick, Jr., *Conquering Loneliness* (Waco: Word, 1979), p. 68.
2. William Proctor, "The Gospel According to Gallup" (*Christian Herald*), November, 1979, p. 60. Italics mine.
3. Karl Menninger, *Whatever Became of Sin?* (New York: Hawthorn, 1973).
4. William James, *The Varieties of Religious Experience* (Garden City, NY: Dolphin/Doubleday, 1902), p. 17.
5. Dawson McAllister, "Misery in the 'Me' Generation" (*Worldwide Challenge*, February, 1980), p. 5.
6. For an analysis of modern selfism, see Vitz, Paul C., *Psychology As Religion: The Cult of Self-Worship* (Grand Rapids: Eerdmans, 1977).
7. Keith Miller, *The Taste of New Wine* (Waco, TX: Word, 1965), p. 97.
8. This term was suggested by Vitz, *Psychology As Religion*, p. 94.
9. This term has been suggested by William Sloan Coffin, Jr.
10. Alexander Solzhenitsyn, *A World Split Apart*. Commencement address delivered at Harvard University, June 8, 1979.

11. See John W. Montgomery, "Evangelical Social Responsibility in Theological Perspective." *Our Society in Turmoil*, ed. Gary R. Collins, (Carol Stream, IL: Creation House, 1970), pp. 13–23.
12. J. I. Packer, *God Has Spoken* (Downers Grove, IL: InterVarsity Press, 1979), p. 20.
13. Pierre Berton, *The Comfortable Pew* (Philadelphia: Lippincott, 1965).
14. Eugene H. Peterson, *A Long Obedience in the Same Direction* (Downers Grove, IL: InterVarsity Press, 1980), p. 12.
15. Solzhenitsyn, *A World Split Apart*.

Chapter 2

1. John Lahr, "Notes on Fame" (*Harper's*, January, 1978), p. 77.
2. A thought-provoking critique of "celebrityism" is contained in Jon Johnston's perceptive book, *Will Evangelicalism Survive Its Own Popularity?* (Grand Rapids: Zondervan, 1980).
3. W. D. Moen, "The Back Door: Our Readers Write," *Wittenburg Door*, December 1978–January 1979, pp. 8–9.
4. Ibid.
5. Ted W. Engstrom and Edward R. Dayton, "God's Purpose or People's Plans," *Christian Leadership Letter*. June, 1980.
6. John W. Gardner, *Excellence* (New York: Harper & Row, 1961), pp. 148, 149.
7. Henry Fairlie, "Too Rich for Heroes," *Harpers*, November, 1978, p. 33.
8. Dietrich Bonhoeffer, *The Cost of Discipleship* (New York: Macmillan, 1973) (1937), pp. 47, 54–55.
9. David G. Myers, *The Human Puzzle: Psychological Research and Christian Belief* (New York: Harper & Row, 1978), p. 134.
10. Douglas Hooker, *The Healthy Personality and the Christian Life* (North Quincy, MA: Christopher, 1977), p. 83.
11. Ibid., p. 84.
12. Engstrom and Dayton, p. 1.
13. The ideas in this section are taken from Richard J. Foster's *Freedom of Simplicity* (New York: Harper & Row, 1981), pp. 92–93.
14. Elton Trueblood, *The Incendiary Fellowship* (New York: Harper & Row, 1967), p. 15.
15. See Elizabeth O'Conner, *Call to Commitment* (New York: Harper & Row, 1963) and Elton Trueblood, *The Company of the Committed* (New York: Harper & Row, 1961).
16. J. I. Packer, *God Has Spoken* (Downers Grove, IL: InterVarsity, 1979), pp. 41–42.
17. Merold Westphal, "Kierkegaard and the Logic of Insanity," (*Religious Studies*, 1971), 204.
18. Bonhoeffer, p. 69.
19. David Roper, *The Law That Sets You Free* (Waco: Word, 1977), p. 39.
20. Richard Foster, *Celebration of Discipline* (New York: Harper & Row, 1978), p. 117.
21. The ideas in this lengthy sentence are major themes discussed in chapters 2–4 of the Book of James.

22. David J. Frenchak, "Religious Porn." *SCUPE Newsletter*, Vol. 3, No. 1, January, 1981.

Chapter 3

1. This summary of the work of G. Stanley Hall is taken from Edwin G. Boring's monumental *History of Experimental Psychology* 2nd ed. (New York: Appleton-Century. Crofts, 1950), pp. 517–524.
2. John R. W. Stott, *Your Mind Matters* (Downers Grove, IL: InterVarsity, 1972), pp. 8–10.
3. Ibid., p. 9.
4. Richard F. Lovelace, *Dynamics of Spiritual Life: An Evangelical Theology of Renewal* (Downers Grove, IL: InterVarsity, 1979), p. 265.
5. Irving L. Janis. *Victims of Groupthink* (Atlanta: Houghton Mifflin, 1972).
6. Clark H. Pinnock. *Reason Enough: A Case for the Christian Faith* (Downers Grove, IL: InterVarsity, 1980), p. 12.
7. Stott, p. 26.
8. See, for example, Pinnock's *Reason Enough* and an earlier book *Set Forth Your Case: An Examination of Christianity's Credentials.* (Chicago: Moody, 1971); F. F. Bruce, *The Defense of the Gospel in the New Testament* (Grand Rapids: Eerdmans, 1959); A. J. Hoover, *The Case for Christian Theism* (Grand Rapids: Baker, 1976); Josh McDowell; *More Than a Carpenter* (Wheaton: Tyndale, 1977).
9. Paul Welter, *How to Help a Friend* (Wheaton: Tyndale, 1977), pp. 88–96.
10. See two books by Josh McDowell, both published by Campus Crusade for Christ, Arrowhead Springs, San Bernandino, California. *Evidence That Demands a Verdict* was published in 1972; *More Evidence That Demands a Verdict* appeared in 1975.
11. *Beyond Freedom and Dignity* (New York: Knopf, 1971) is the title of a widely read and controversial book by B. F. Skinner, a man who is perhaps the best-known humanistic psychologist.
12. James I. Packer, *Knowing Man* (Westchester, IL: Cornerstone, 1978), p. 13.
13. Pinnock, p. 118.
14. Ibid., p. 108.
15. Ibid.
16. In these paragraphs space does not permit the citing of data. Please see footnote 8 for statements of data.
17. Pinnock, p. 38.
18. "Islam vs. Christianity: Josh McDowell debates a Muslim apologist in South Africa." *Worldwide Challenge*, November, 1981, pp. 40–41.
19. See F. F. Bruce, *The New Testament Documents: Are They Reliable?* (Grand Rapids: Eerdmans, 1943).

Chapter 4

1. An old but widely acclaimed discussion of the emotions of Jesus can be seen in a chapter titled "On the Emotional Life of our Lord," in Benjamin B. Warfield, *The Person and Work of Christ* (Philadelphia: Presbyterian and Reformed, 1950), pp. 93–95.

2. Daniel Yankelovich. "New Rules in American Life." *Psychology Today.* Vol. 15, (April 1981), p. 80.
3. For a more detailed analysis of these issues, see Jim McFadden, "Feeling Your Way into Bondage: On the Uninhibited Exploring and Sharing of Feelings." *Pastoral Renewal,* February, 1980, Vol. 4. (Available from Pastoral Renewal, 840 Airport Blvd., P.O. Box 8617, Ann Arbor, Michigan, 48107).
4. As examples see Lloyd H. Ahlem, *How to Cope* (Ventura, CA: Regal, 1978); Barry Applewhite, *Feeling Good About Your Feelings* (Wheaton, IL: Victor Books, 1980); David Augsburger, *Caring Enough to Confront* (Rev. ed.) (Ventura, CA: Regal, 1980); Gary Collins, *Overcoming Anxiety* (Santa Ana, CA: Vision House, 1973); Gary Collins, *Calm Down* (Chappaqua, N.Y.: Christian Herald,* 1981); James Dobson, *Emotions: Can You Trust Them?* (Ventura, CA: Regal, 1980); Archibald Hart, *Feeling Free* (Old Tappan, N.J.: Revell, 1980); Robert L. Wise, *Your Churning Place* (Ventura, CA: Regal, 1977); and H. Norman Wright, *The Christian Use of Emotional Power* (Old Tappan, N.J.: Revell, 1974).
5. Ronald L. Kotesky, "Toward the Development of a Christian Psychology: Emotion." *Journal of Psychology and Theology.* Winter, 1980, Vol. 8, pp. 303–313.
6. P. T. Young, *Emotion in Man and Aminal* (2nd rev. ed.) (Huntington, N.Y.: Krieger, 1973).
7. Kotesky, p. 303.
8. Each of us, I suspect, could come up with a personal listing of such books. Among others, I would include William H. Whyte's *The Organization Man* (1957); Vance Parker's *The Hidden Persuaders* (1981); and Alvin Toffler's *Future Shock* (1970).
9. Published by Random House, New York, 1981.
10. Yankelovich, "New Rules," p. 36.
11. Ibid., p. 47.
12. Erich Fromm, *The Sane Society* (New York: Rinehart, 1955), pp. 36–38.
13. Peter Marin. "Living in Moral Pain." *Psychology Today,* November, 1981, Vol. 15, p. 74.
14. Ibid., p. 80.

Chapter 5

1. D. Martyn Lloyd-Jones, *Studies in the Sermon on the Mount* (Grand Rapids: Eerdmans, 1959–1960), p. 18.
2. John R. W. Stott, *Christian Counter-Culture: The Message of the Sermon on the Mount.* (Downers Grove, IL: InterVarsity, 1978), p. 19.
3. R. V. G. Tasker, *The Gospel According to St. Matthew* (Grand Rapids: Eerdmans, 1961), p. 63.
4. Stott, p. 60.
5. These purposes are proposed by William Barclay, *The Gospel of Matthew* (vol. 1, rev. ed.) (Philadelphia: Westminster, 1975), pp. 123–125.
6. Stott, pp. 59, 60.
7. James Packer, *Fundamentalism and the Word of God* (Downers Grove, IL: InterVarsity, 1958).

8. Richard Quebedeaux, *The Worldly Evangelicals.* (New York: Harper & Row, 1978), pp. 12–14.

9. Harry Blamires, *Where Do We Stand?* (Ann Arbor: Servant Books, 1980), p. 12.

10. Kenneth S. Wuest, *Romans in the Greek New Testament* (Grand Rapids: Eerdmans, 1955), p. 205.

11. Charles M. Sheldon, *In His Steps.* (Chicago: Advance Publishing Co., 1896).

Chapter 6

1. This quotation from Anatole de Laforge is included in Michael Korda's book *Success!* (New York: Bantam Books [Iainu Research Corporation], 1977), p. vi.

2. This is the view of W. Somerset Maugham, also recorded in Korda, ibid., p. 2.

3. Korda, p. 3.

4. Joan L. Guest, *We Are Driven: The Success Syndrome and How it Affects You. His,* Vol. 49. October, 1979, p. 1.

5. Richard Lovelace, *Dynamics of Spiritual Renewal* (Downer's Grove, IL: Inter-Varsity, 1979), pp. 151, 205.

6. David G. Myers and Jack Ridl, "Can We all be Better than Average?" *Psychology Today.* Vol. 13, August, 1979, pp. 89–98.

7. Daniel Yankelovich, "Who Gets Ahead in America" *Psychology Today.* Vol. 13. July, 1979, pp. 28–34, 40–43, 90–91.

8. John W. Gardner, *Excellence* (New York: Harper & Row, 1961), p. 18.

9. Ibid., p. 147.

10. Ibid., p. 86.

11. Richard J. Foster, *Celebration of Discipline: The Path to Spiritual Growth* (New York: Harper & Row), 1978, p. 1.

12. John E. Gardner, *Personal Religious Disciplines* (Grand Rapids: Eerdmans, 1966), p. 13.

13. Jean Cadier, *The Man God Mastered* (London: InterVarsity, 1960).

14. William Barclay, *The Letters of James and Peter* (Philadelphia: Westminster, 1958), p. 356.

15. Ibid., p. 357.

16. Ibid., pp. 358–59.

17. Ted Engstrom, "Goals that Mobilize." *Pastoral Renewal.* October, 1980, vol. 5, pp. 27–29. The next several paragraphs are adapted from Engstrom's informative and practical article.

18. Ibid., p. 29.

19. Henri J. M. Nouwen, *The Genesee Diary: Report from a Trappist Monastery* (Garden City, New York: Doubleday Image Books, 1981), p. 14.

20. Ibid., pp. 77–78.

Chapter 7

1. Erich Fromm, *The Art of Loving* (New York: Bantam, 1963).

2. Ibid., p. vii.

3. George Sweeting, *Love Is the Greatest* (rev. ed.) (Chicago: Moody Press, 1974), p. 21.

4. Ibid., p. 22.
5. Fromm, pp. 38–69.
6. G. B. Funderburk, "Love," in Merrill C. Tenney, (ed.) *The Zondervan Pictoral Encyclopedia of the Bible* (vol. 3.) (Grand Rapids: Zondervan, 1975), pp. 989–96.
7. C. S. Lewis, *The Four Loves* (London: Geoffrey Bles, 1960).
8. Sweeting, p. 27.
9. Funderburk, p. 989.
10. Ibid.
11. Charles R. Swindoll, *Improving Your Serve: The Art of Unselfish Living* (Waco, TX: Word, 1981), p. 162.
12. William Barclay, *The Gospel of Matthew* (vol. 2), (rev. ed.) Philadelphia: Westminster, 1975, p. 229.
13. Ibid., p. 13.
14. John F. Alexander. "I Don't Want to be a Servant," *The Other Side*, (Vol. 17), March, 1981, pp. 10–13.
15. Ibid., p. 13.
16. Swindoll, p. 12.
17. Ibid., pp. 12, 13.
18. Ibid., p. 25.
19. D. Martyn Lloyd-Jones, *Studies in the Sermon on the Mount* (Grand Rapids: Eerdmans, 1959), p. 35.
20. William Barclay, *The Gospel of Matthew* (vol. 1), (rev. ed.) (Philadelphia: Westminster, 1975), p. 98.
21. Swindoll, pp. 42–80.
22. Barclay, pp. 109, 110.
23. Swindoll, p. 118.
24. John R. W. Stott, *Christian Counter-Culture* (Downers Grove: InterVarsity, 1978), p. 54.
25. Ibid., p. 56.
26. Barclay, p. 111.
27. John A. T. Robinson, *Honest to God* (Philadelphia: Westminster, 1963).
28. H. Richard Niebuhr, *Christ and Culture* (New York: Harper & Row, 1961).
29. See, for example, Ronald J. Sider, *Cry Justice* (Downers Grove: InterVarsity, 1980).
30. Mark O. Hatfield, "Finding the Energy to Continue," *Christianity Today*. Vol. 34. February 8, 1980, pp. 20–24.
31. The term is that of Francis A. Schaeffer, *The Church at the End of the 20th Century* (Downers Grove: InterVarsity, 1970), Appendix II.

Chapter 8

1. The quotations and most of the conclusions about Puritanism in this chapter were taken from an article by Leland Ryken. "Were the Puritans Right About Sex?" in *Christianity Today*, vol. 22, April 7, 1978, pp. 13–16. I am grateful to Dr. John Woodbridge, Professor of Church History at Trinity Evangelical Divinity School, for checking the historical accuracy of this discussion of the Puritans.

2. Ibid., p. 16.
3. Charlie and Martha Shedd, *Celebration in the Bedroom* (Waco, TX: Word, 1979) p. 11. The idea of sex as something to celebrate also appears in the title of a book by Dwight Hervey Small, *Christian Celebrate Your Sexuality: A Fresh, Positive Approach to Understanding and Fulfilling Sexuality* (Old Tappan, N.J.: Revell, 1974).
4. Shedd, p. 89.
5. Consider, for example, a book by Ed and Gaye Wheat, *Intended for Pleasure* (Old Tappan, N.J.: Revell, 1977). Also helpful is Tim and Beverly LaHaye, *The Act of Marriage: The Beauty of Sexual Love* (Grand Rapids: Zondervan, 1976). For a sensitive Christian discussion of sexual tensions and issues such as premarital sex, masturbation, and homosexuality, see John White's *Eros Defiled: The Christian and Sexual Sin* (Downers Grove, IL: InterVarsity, 1977).
6. John Calvin, *Institutes of the Christian Religion, Book One of the Knowledge of God the Creator* (MacDill, Florida: MacDonald, 1973), p. 7.
7. Ibid., p. 8.
8. Ibid.
9. A. W. Tozer, *The Knowledge of the Holy: The Attributes of God: Their Meaning in the Christian Life* (New York: Harper and Row, 1961).
10. Ibid., p. 110.
11. This section is adapted from Richard C. Lovelace, *Dynamics of Spiritual Life* (Downers Grove, IL: InterVarsity, 1979).
12. This idea of society's changing the terms to make perverse sexual acts more palatable is noted by Michael Braun and George Alan Rekers in *The Christian in an Age of Sexual Eclipse* (Wheaton: Tyndale, 1981), pp. 34–39.
13. C. S. Lewis, *The Screwtape Letters.* (Glasgow: Collins, 1942), p. 9.
14. Lovelace, pp. 137–140.
15. Ibid., p. 139.
16. James Robison, *Attack on the Family* (Wheaton: Tyndale, 1980), p. 26.
17. This is the title of an excellent volume by Walter Trobisch, *Living with Unfulfilled Desires* (Downers Grove, IL: InterVarsity, 1979).
18. D. G. Kehl. "Sneaky Stimuli and How to Resist Them." *Christianity Today.* January 31, 1975, p. 10.
19. Ibid. See also Wilson Bryan Key's *Subliminal Seduction: Ad Media's Manipulation of a Not So Innocent America* (New York: Prentice Hall, 1973).
20. Kehl, p. 10.
21. This conclusion is reached by Anthony Brandt, "What It Means to Say No." *Psychology Today,* vol. 15, (August, 1981), pp. 70–77.
22. This is the title of a book by Manuel J. Smith, *When I Say No I Feel Guilty* (New York: Bantam Books, 1975).
23. Brandt, "What It Means to Say No."

Chapter 9

1. See, for example, "The Traditional Family Will Make a Comeback: Interview with Dr. Lee Salk, Child Psychologist" *U. S. News and World Report,* June 16, 1980, pp. 60–61.

2. The Gallup Organization, *American Families, 1980*. Report submitted to the White House Conference on Families by the Gallup Organization. Princeton, N.J.: Gallup, 1980, p. 3.
3. Kathleen B. Bryer, "The Amish Way of Death: A Study of Family Support Systems." *American Psychologist*. March, 1979, pp. 255–261.
4. Cited in Armand M. Nicholi II, "The Fractured Family: Following It into the Future," *Christianity Today*. May 25, 1979, p. 13.
5. Ibid.
6. H. Gray Watson in a personal conversation.
7. The President's Commission for a National Agenda for the Eighties. "Helping Families—To Help Themselves." *International Journal of Family Therapy*. Fall, 1981, pp. 208–233.
8. Urie Bronfenbrenner, "The Origins of Alienation." *Scientific American*, August, 1974.
9. For a statement of the view that the family is being deliberately undermined see James Robison, *Attack on the Family* (Wheaton: Tyndale House, 1980).
10. Jack Mabley. "TV: Bigger Peril than Atomic Bomb." *Chicago Tribune*, August 11, 1976.
11. Quoted (but without approval) in O. R. Johnston, *Who Needs the Family?* Downers Grove, IL: InterVarsity, 1979, p. 138.
12. "Son of Abraham" was a common rabbinic title for a good man. It was unheard of to describe a woman as a "daughter of Abraham." See Michael Braun and George Rekers, *The Christian in an Age of Sexual Eclipse* (Wheaton: Tyndale, 1981), p. 153. I have drawn heavily on these authors in writing this section of the book. See also Stephen B. Clark, *Man and Woman in Christ: An Examination of the Roles of Men and Women in Light of Scripture and the Social Sciences* (Ann Arbor: Servant Books, 1980).
13. Braun and Rekers, *Sexual Eclipse*, p. 183.
14. Ibid.
15. This view is expressed more fully in Herbert M. Greenberg, *Coping with Job Stress* (Englewood Cliffs, N.J.: Prentice-Hall, 1980).
16. C. S. Lewis, *The Screwtape Letters* (London: Collins Fontana Books, 1942).
17. Gerald L. Dahl, *Why Christian Marriages Are Breaking Up* (Nashville: Nelson, 1979).
18. Portions of this section are adapted from an article by the author, Gary R. Collins "The Christian Family—Building a Better Future." *The Evangelical Beacon*. 54, April 15, 1981, pp. 4–6.
19. For a further discussion of family clusters see Del and Trudy Vander Haar, "Family Cluster Education." In Gary R. Collins (ed.) *Facing the Future: The Church and Family Together* (Waco, TX: Word, 1976), pp. 43–59.

Chapter 10

1. Chapel talk delivered by President Mortvedt, May 13, 1963, printed in *Reflections*, Pacific Northern University Bulletin, October, 1964.
2. Some of this discussion is taken from an article by Bernard R. Ramm, "Is It Safe to Shift to 'Interpersonal Theology?'" *Eternity*. December, 1972, pp. 21–22.

3. Personal communication.
4. Bruce Larson, *The Relational Revolution* (Waco, TX: Word, 1976), pp. 84–85.
5. Richard J. Foster, *Celebration of Discipline* (New York: Harper & Row, 1978), p. 140.
6. Alfred A. Glenn, *Taking Your Faith to Work* (Grand Rapids: Baker, 1980), p. 32.
7. Ibid.
8. A. W. Tozer, *The Knowledge of the Holy* (New York: Harper & Row, 1961), pp. 6, 7.
9. Jerry Custer, "Worship—Our Response to the God Who Acts," *Pastoral Renewal*, December, 1981, pp. 44–46.
10. Ibid.
11. Ibid.
12. Charles Merrill Smith, *How to Become a Bishop without Being Religious* (Garden City, NY: Doubleday, 1965).
13. Foster, *Celebration*, p. 148.
14. John E. Gardner, *Personal Religious Disciplines* (Grand Rapids: Eerdmans, 1966), p. 87.
15. From the Preface to Brother Lawrence's *The Practice of the Presence of God* (Old Tappan, N.J.: Revell [Spire Books], 1958).
16. P. T. Forsyth, *The Soul of Prayer* (5th ed.) (London: Independent Press, 1966), p. 11.
17. This is the theme of a book by Donald G. Bloesch, *The Struggle of Prayer* (San Francisco: Harper & Row, 1980).
18. John Calvin, *Sermons on the Epistle to the Ephesians* (Edinburgh: Banner of Truth Trust, 1975), p. 682.
19. Henri J. M. Nouwen, *Clowning in Rome* (Garden City, NY: Doubleday-Image, 1979), p. 21.
20. G. W. Bromiley, "Worship" *The Zondervan Pictorial Encyclopedia of the Bible.* (vol. 5), Merrill C. Tenney, General Editor, (Grand Rapids: Zondervan, 1975).
21. Malcolm Muggeridge, *Something Beautiful for God: Mother Teresa of Calcutta* (Garden City, NY: Doubleday [Image Books], 1971), pp. 16, 100.

Chapter 11

1. Edith Weisskopf-Joelson, "Some Comments on a Viennese School of Psychiatry" *The Journal of Abnormal and Social Psychology*, Vol. 51, 1955, pp. 701–3.
2. Viktor E. Frankl, *Man's Search for Meaning* (New York: Washington Square Press, 1959), p. 164.
3. Malcolm Muggeridge, *The End of Christendom* (Grand Rapids: Eerdmans, 1980), pp. 22, 17, 18, 19–20.
4. Ibid., pp. 52–53.
5. Ibid., p. 56.
6. Elisabeth Kubler-Ross, *On Death and Dying* (New York: Macmillan, 1969).
7. Ibid., pp. 123–24.

8. Reported by Bill Roth. "Where Is Your Hope?" *Worldwide Challenge.* August, 1980, pp. 5–7.
9. Ibid.
10. Gary R. Collins, *Christian Counseling* (Waco, TX: Word, 1980), p. 53.
11. Keith Miller, *The Taste of New Wine* (Waco, TX: Word, 1965), pp. 22, 27.
12. Reported in William Barclay, *The Letters to the Corinthians* (Edinburgh: St. Andrews Press, 1954), p. 210.
13. Hans Selye, *The Stress of Life* (New York: McGraw-Hill, 1956).
14. Ibid., pp. 284, 285.
15. Ibid., p. 286.

Index

Study Guide

Chapter 1

1. Does contemporary music—like the music of John Lennon—reflect the attitudes and thinking of a culture like ours? Can you think of some examples? What does music say about our country, our values, our churches, our families?

2. Can you give your own definition of easy believism? On the assumption that each of us falls into easy believism at times, list some of the evidences of easy believism in your life.

3. The Epistle of James warns against worthless religion. Is your religion worthless? Is it a dull habit? Is it really meaningful? Be honest. How does James 1:27, 28 apply to you?

4. On an airplane one day, the author was asked, "Do you know what it means to be born again?" How would you answer? Be specific.

Chapter 2

1. Do you agree with the view that we have encouraged celebrityism within our churches? Is this bad?

2. The chapter begins with a quotation from Luke 9:23. How can this verse apply to your life? Try to be specific in your answer.

3. What is your reaction to the following quotations: Do you agree or disagree? Why?

    a. "The best kept secret in America today is that people would rather work hard for something they believe in than enjoy a pampered idleness." (p. 33)

    b. "Only he who believes is obedient, and only he who is obedient believes." (p. 40)

4. A lot of people admire Corrie ten Boom. If she was your age and living in your community today, how would she show her commitment to Christ? What does this say about you?

Chapter 3

1. What is the difference between nothink, shallowthink, and groupthink? Have you seen these forms of thinking in your church or in your own life? Can you think of examples? What is a better alternative?

2. Five questions appear at the top of page 52. How would you answer each of them? Where could you get further information about the answers to these questions?

3. Please look at the church on page 53. Where do you fit? What are your strong and weak channels? How does this knowledge strengthen your relationship to Christ?

4. Think about this question: "How can I be like God unless I really understand what God is like?" What are you doing to really understand what God is like? What else could you do?

Chapter 4

1. What is the meaning of feelingless stoicism, unrestrained emotionalism, and psychological subjectivism? Which of these tendencies is most prevalent in your life? How could your emotional life be more healthy and consistent with biblical teaching?

2. Page 68 gives several guidelines for self-control. Can you think of an example in your life where this formula has helped or could help with self-control? What other steps could you take to control emotions? Try to be specific.

3. Is it possible to be too introspective? Do you agree that excessive introspection can destroy intimacy and bring both loneliness and depression? How can excessive introspection hinder your spiritual growth? What are specific steps you can take this week to avoid excessive introspection?

4. What is moral pain? Can you think of a personal example? How can this be handled in your life? Read 1 John 1:8, 9. What do you do if you confess your sins to God but still don't feel forgiven? Read James 5:16.

Chapter 5

1. Ghandi once said, "My life is my message." When people look at your life style, what kind of a message do they get about your beliefs and values? Do you want to make changes in your life style? How will you do this? When?

2. Do you agree with the man who concluded that nobody can live in accordance with the Sermon on the Mount and survive in our modern society? Look over Matthew 5, 6, and 7 before you answer.

3. In what ways are you a fundamentalist? Notice the author's description of new fundamentalism. Which of these characteristics apply to you?

4. In making decisions about your actions and life style, is it really helpful to ask, "What would Jesus do in this situation?" Is Col. 1:10 a realistic guideline for daily living?

5. Are the guidelines on page 90–91 really helpful? Think of some specific characteristic of your life style. How could these guidelines be applied?

Chapter 6

1. What represents success for you? Be honest: if you could have every evidence of success in this life, what would your life be like?

2. Can we be successful in God's eyes but unsuccessful in the eyes of other people? Would you really be willing for that to characterize your life? How can Matt. 20:25–8 apply to you?

3. On page 97, the author gives a description of the successful Christian. Do you agree with this description? What would you add or subtract from the list?

4. Do you agree with the characteristics of greatness listed in this chapter? How do you measure up in terms of this list?

5. Are the four guidelines on pages 106–110 really practical? Perhaps you would be willing to apply this formula to your own life. Plan to give a report on your progress to some friend within a week.

Chapter 7

1. Give your own definition of love. In view of the scriptural teaching in 1 John 4:8 and 12, how do you account for the fact that so many Christians seem to be lacking in love? How do you account for the lack of love in your life?

2. Please read Matt. 5:3–12. Is it really possible to be a servant at your work, in your home, or in your neighborhood? How would this work out in practice?

3. In light of 2 Tim. 3:12, do you really believe that the Christian in our society should expect persecution? How can you prepare for persecution?

4. Assume that Niebuhr is right: the Christian is a transformer of culture. How can you do this? Be specific. See John 13:34, 35.

Chapter 8

1. Were you surprised by the author's discussion of Puritanism? How can we be true Puritans today?

2. Are you guilty of the "habituation" described on page 128? How could you change, without becoming rigid or insensitive?

3. What is your reaction to the following statements?
   a. "True and solid wisdom consists almost entirely of two parts: the knowledge of God and of ourselves. . . . Man never attains to true self-knowledge until he has previously contemplated the face of God and come down after such contemplation to look at himself." (p. 130)
   b. "The best way to maintain sexual purity is to ponder the characteristics of God." (p. 130)
   c. "The Christian's victory over seduction lies in the indwelling Word of God and the indwelling Spirit of God." (pp. 136–7)

4. Look at the five strategies of Satan described on pages 132–5. Which of these have you seen in your life? What can you do about them? Look at James 4:7; 1 John 1:9; 4:4; Eph. 6:10–18.

5. How can Romans 12:1 and 2 help you to live a life of sanctified sexuality?

Chapter 9

1. Think back over the past few years of your life. In what ways has your family changed? What are the strong and weak areas of your family life today? Based on your reading of this chapter, in what ways can you change to improve your family?

2. Read Eph. 5:21–6:4. How do you respond to this portion of God's Word? Be honest. How can *you* change to more accurately conform to the biblical guidelines for family living?

3. On pages 147–9 the author lists eight common "mentalities" which adversely affect family living. Which of these are in you? What would you add to this list? In what ways can you change your thinking in order to improve family life? Please try to be specific.

4. Do you agree that "families need other families for mutual encouragement and support?" How does this apply to the church? How does it apply to you and to your family?

Chapter 10

1. How do you worship God, alone and/or with others? What attitudes do you bring to worship? Based on your reading of this chapter, what could you do to make worship more significant?

2. Think about the worship services in your church. How could these be changed to make them more honoring to God and more meaningful to the congregation?

3. Think about your prayer life. Are you one of those Christians who spends no more than 10 minutes a day in prayer and meditation on the Scriptures? What could you do to change? Be specific. What will you do differently during the coming week?

4. Re-read this quotation from page 164 of the book. Ponder how it applies to your life: Our regular periods of solitude must be supplemented, periodically, by extra times for communication with God. An evening or half-day of prayer, a weekend alone, a time of prayer with one's family or a trusted friend—these can all pay rich dividends in terms of added spiritual vigor.

5. "Ask not what can my church do for me, but ask what can I do for my church." What kind of a response does this statement arouse in you?

Chapter 11

1. Think about your life. Do you really have hope? If not, why not? How can you develop a more hope-filled life?

2. What is your response to these statements:

a. "Because I know the Who, I can endure the what, even without knowing the why." (p. 172)

b. "In the final analysis . . . gratitude and revenge are the most important factors governing our actions in everyday life; upon them also chiefly depend our peace of mind, our feelings of security or insecurity, of fulfillment, or frustration, in short, the extent to which we can make a success of life." (p. 178)

3. Do you wear a mask of spirituality? How can you change to experience the hope and radiance of true communion with God? Once again, please try to be specific in your answer.

4. How could you answer the four questions with which the book ends on page 180?